ARE YOU
Spirit Led
or
Emotionally
Driven?

Maureen Anderson

FOREWORD BY
PAULA WHITE

Winword
publishing house

Phoenix, Arizona

FIRST EDITION

   Published by **Winword Publishing, Inc.**
   3520 E. Brown Road, Mesa, AZ 85213
   (480) 964-4GOD

   ISBN 1-58588-135-X

Are You Spirit-Led or Emotionally-Driven?

Office number for book orders:

   1-888-4WORDTV (1-888-496-7388)

or visit **www.winners.tv**

Printed in Canada

Cover Photography by: Brad Sandoval
                          Looking Good Photography of Arizona

Cover Design by: Derek Jordan
                          One Source Graphic Design Inc.

Table of Contents

Dedication

I dedicate this book to my very best friend, the man of my dreams, who believes in me and supports me completely in all that I do—my husband.

I dedicate this book to my children, Scot, Holly, Jason and Kelli, who have always made me feel that I could do anything in Christ, and have made life worth living for me.

I dedicate this book to my seven grandchildren who are the joy of grandma.

Foreword
by Paula White

Two natures beat within my breast.
One is cursed. One is blessed.
One I love, one I hate.
The one I feed will dominate.
(Author unknown)

The battle of flesh and Spirit goes back to the beginning of time. Since man's very origins, we have been fighting that which we "feel" versus that which we know to be true based on the Spirit of God that resides within us. How many times have you said something you wish you could take back or done something out of spite or anxiety that later brought you shame or disappointment? It's not that we are bad people or want to do evil. Flesh operates on a system of taking, while the Spirit gives. If given the opportunity, your flesh will always convince you that someone "owes" you something or is trying to take away what is rightfully yours. In contrast, the Spirit is fully aware that what God has for you is for you. It does not fight or steal or cause conflict in order to win.

Emotions are a crucial part of your flesh. They often drive your attitude, speech and actions. From the Old Testament to the New Testament, there are countless examples of men and women of God who allowed their emotions to determine their destiny. From Eve to the Apostle Paul, we are shown great examples of people who loved God, and had the best of intentions, yet struggled to win the battle between the two natures.

Take heed. Emotions can control every part of who you are—if you allow them to. Mastering the art of yielding to the Spirit and constantly crucifying the flesh is the key to living the life of abundance that God has for you.

The Holy Spirit is gentle and loving. He will never ever push you in any direction. He will lovingly advise, or convict if there is sin. Think about the contrast of your emotions. They are forceful and unrelenting, pushing you to act or react before fully thinking through potential consequences.

One of the final statements that Jesus made while on the cross was to His mother. In John 19, He instructs His mother that the disciple standing nearby is now her son, and He tells the disciple to take His mother as his own. Many skip over this portion of scripture, or make the quick assumption that Jesus was merely looking out for the future care of His mother. This is true, but not completely. There is another layer to this scripture. In essence, He was saying: "Go home, Mama, and let me do the will of God." Jesus recognized at that moment that Mary, the part of Him that was flesh, had to be separated, cut off. You have to face the issue of the flesh in your life—the thing that can and will keep you from doing the will of God—before you can walk out the full manifestation of what God has created for you.

In Taking Charge of Your Emotions, Pastor Maureen Anderson delves into the age-old topic of being Spirit-led and not emotionally-driven. Read every word as if your destiny depended upon it. It just might!

Paula White

Introduction

We live in a very emotional world. Every day the news is filled with stories of people who are driven by their emotions to do crazy and destructive things. Emotions have a great impact on our lives every day. When they are positive emotions, we really enjoy them. When they are not, we suffer because of them. But we all feel them, either way.

The problem is that our daily lives are dictated by those emotions. We react to them. Our behavior is created out of them. Most people are emotionally-driven. Most people think that they have no control.

But the Bible says that it should be different. God says that we should be led by the Holy Spirit. Instead of being emotionally-driven, we are to be Spirit-led.

It is for this reason that I want to share with you what God has taught me about harnessing my emotions and bringing them into submission to the Spirit of God. It is a process of mastering your emotions rather than letting them master you.

When you are Spirit-led, you learn to separate the spirit from the soul. You learn to tie your emotions to Scripture, to what God says, rather than just what you feel.

It is a matter of learning self-awareness by the Holy Spirit so that you recognize when the adrenaline is flowing and you make a plan to bring it under control before it does harm.

It is a matter of learning to purposely place your emotions where God says they should be so that they will serve the purpose for which God created them and bring you into the joyful and victorious life that God always wanted for you, so that your emotions become a positive link to faith.

My purpose is to share with you how to live in the promises of God rather than being tossed about by every circumstance. My goal is to see you enjoy your life, your family and your destiny.

1
Set Your Affections

But the fruit of the Spirit is love, joy, peace, patience, kindness, goodness, faithfulness, gentleness and self-control. Against such things there is no law. (Galatians 5:22-23)

The key to controlling our emotions is to bring them into submission to the Holy Spirit. When we do that, we are training our emotions to come into line with the emotions of God. It is my emotions embracing the emotions of the Holy Spirit, to be taught by the Holy Spirit, to be in agreement with the Holy Spirit. We begin to feel the emotions that God wants us to feel and they become productive in our lives instead of destructive. It should be our goal to take on the same emotions that God has and let them flow through our emotions.

The first step is to stop blaming God or your parents or your circumstances for your emotions and your behavior. They are not responsible. Who is the one responsible? James tells us that we are.

When tempted, no one should say, "God is tempting me." For God cannot be tempted by

evil, nor does he tempt anyone; but each one
is tempted when, by his own evil desire, he is
dragged away and enticed. Then, after desire
has conceived, it gives birth to sin; and sin,
when it is full-grown, gives birth to death.
(James 1:13-15)

It is our own evil desires that lead us away.
The truth is that our emotions, when they drive
our behavior, result in bad choices that lead us
away from the place God wants us to be. We cannot blame God. We have to take responsibility for
our own choices. If we do not, then we stay in the
prison that our uncontrolled emotions have created for us.

We will discuss various negative emotions and
how we can rein them in, get rid of the bad ones
and develop the good ones. There are a wide va-
riety of them, such as anger, fear, sadness, anxiety
and stress. Before you can deal with any of them,
however, you absolutely must stop blaming God for
the bad things in your life. It is essential that you
acknowledge that God is good and that He has good
in mind for you. He wants you to experience emotions that give you life and joy and that bring you
into the love walk. He wants you free of the bond-
age and restraints that uncontrolled emotions bring
into your life. God wants the Spirit in control, not
your emotions.

What are the emotions of God? We can see them in the fruit of the Holy Spirit. We should notice that when we are Spirit-led and we live in His emotions, we are not under the law. We do not need the law because our emotions are guided, tamed and directed by the Spirit. We have them inside of us to draw on and to embrace, instead of emotions that are out of control and destructive. "The love of God is shed abroad in our hearts by the Holy Ghost" (Romans 5:5 KJV). That means that we have the emotion of love the same way that God does; I have His love. His joy is in me (John 16:24). I have His peace (Philippians 4:7). I have His goodness. All of these things are by the Holy Spirit. God has put those things in me and when I embrace them, I begin to feel the emotions that go with them.

Choosing the Direction of Your Emotions

How do you do that? The next step is to recognize that you can determine where your emotions go. You can make a decision that will direct your emotions in a godly way. In fact, the Bible tells us to do just that.

> *Set your affection on things above, not on things on the earth. For ye are dead, and your life is hid with Christ in God.* (Colossians 3:2, 3 KJV)

You have died. Your life is hidden with Christ. Your life is in God. You need to put your emotions where there is life. If you don't take charge of them and set them in the Kingdom, they will take charge of you instead—and that will be very dangerous. To live a godly life, you must set your affections in the Kingdom of God, not in the things of the world. You can set your affections in any place that you choose. Be sure that you choose the things of God.

It is important to recognize that you are the one who does that. It is not your family or your boss or your neighbor. You are the one who determines where your emotions will be placed. We will return to this thought, but for now, understand that it is one of the most critical actions you can take every day. Just as you cannot say that God tempted you because you are the one who is led away by your own desire, you also have it within your power to choose a different direction for your emotions. You are the one who does it.

We are a spirit and we are to direct our emotions. We are to guide them, to train them and to develop them into what they were created for. The next thing to realize is that choosing emotions is to some degree an act of faith. For example, when you choose to rejoice, but you don't feel like rejoicing, you are calling those things that are not as though they are (Romans 4:17). You are seeing it done.

You are saying, "I receive it now." You are being obedient to God and to what emotion His Word is telling you to choose.

"Faith is the substance of things hoped for, the evidence of things not seen" (Hebrews 11:1 KJV). When you set your affections on things above, on the things of God, you are choosing not to look at what can be seen—that stress (John 14:27), that anxiety (Philippians 4:6-7; 1 Peter 1:6-8), that negative situation—because it is temporal. Instead you are looking at what you don't see because it is eternal (2 Corinthians 4:18). You are walking in faith.

> When you walk in faith, your emotions will work for you, not the other way around.

That is why we rejoice. In faith, we don't allow ourselves to have any negative, unbelieving emotions. This is why Paul said to set our affections on things above where Christ Jesus is seated, not on the things of the earth. That is faith.

When you walk in faith, your emotions will work for you. You are the boss, not your emotions. They are to work for you. If you do not choose to set your emotions in their place every day, they will not work for you. Your emotions will become the boss and you will become the employee. Then, as an employee, you will do whatever your boss, your emotions, tell you to do. That is a dangerous place to be. Your life will manifest the acts of the flesh if you do not harness those emotions, if you do not choose the emotions God tells you to choose. And He always tells you in His Word the right emotion for the situation. What is conceived in your heart is what you will give birth to.

Many times we succumb to wrong emotions simply because we do not make a decision ahead of time. We have not determined how we will behave before we encounter a test. We did not set our emotions in the Kingdom of God. You could be on a date, before you are married, and find yourself in a passionate, powerful emotional moment. A romantic song comes on the radio and all of the sudden, your emotions carry you away and you are doing something you never thought you would ever do. The problem is that you did not make a decision ahead of time to set those emotions on the things of God. You must be proactive.

Do Not Be Anxious

Since the Bible says that it is you who must set your emotions, it is in your power to direct your emotions. You need to start each day by declaring what kind of a day you are going to have. Right from the beginning, wake up in the morning and get excited about that day.

*Make a joyfull shout to the L*ORD*, all you lands!*
*Serve the L*ORD *with gladness;*
Come before His presence with singing.
*Know that the L*ORD*, He is God.*
It is He who has made us, and not we ourselves;
We are His people and the sheep of His pasture.
Enter into His gates with thanksgiving,
And into His courts with praise.
Be thankful to Him, and bless His name.

(Psalm 100:1-4 NKJV)

This is how you create an atmosphere that will promote healthy, godly emotions. You declare it. Make a joyful noise. Choose to rejoice. Choose to serve God with gladness for that day. Choose to enjoy your job and do the best work you can. Choose to enter His gates with thanksgiving.

You direct your emotions by setting your affections on things above. You set your affections by choosing to be proactive from the moment you wake up. You bring your emotions into submission to the Holy Spirit. The Spirit dictates to them where they will be set. You choose not to let your emotions dictate to you. You do it all with gladness and thanksgiving.

Scripture tells us the emotions we should embrace. Peace, love, joy and thankfulness are some of them. But it also tells us emotions that we should say no to.

Do not let your hearts be troubled. Trust in God; trust also in me. (John 14:1)

Another translation says simply, "Don't let yourself be upset." You can say no to turmoil and push it away when trouble comes. When things don't go the way you wanted them to, you don't have to be upset. You can choose not to let your heart be troubled. You do that by setting your affections on the things of God and saying no to stress, upset or trouble. You choose to rejoice instead of being upset.

By setting your emotions on positive things, you leave no room for the unbelieving, negative emotions that speak contrary to God's Word to you. When you embrace joy, there is no place for unbelief. When you embrace peace, there is no room to be upset or anxious. When you embrace wealth, there is no room for poverty. When you embrace health, there is no room for sickness. When you embrace your marriage, there is no place for anything that would destroy that relationship, whether it be abuse, an affair or simple negligence. There's no room left to take offense against your husband or wife. Instead, you live in the commitment to one another to build emotions that strengthen the marriage rather than the emotions that destroy the marriage.

By choosing not to let your heart be troubled, you set your emotions on the things of God.

Paul echoed the command of Jesus when he wrote to the Philippians.

> *Do not be anxious about anything, but in everything, by prayer and petition, with thanksgiving, present your requests to God. And the peace of God, which transcends all understanding, will guard your hearts and your minds in Christ Jesus.* (Philippians 4:6-7)

What will you do when something negative comes along? Often we feel like we owe it to our emotions to have a pity party, to be sad, depressed and down. That is what our emotions demand of us. If you feel that way, however, it means that you are allowing your emotions to tell you how to behave. You are allowing them to be the boss.

The Bible says that you are to decide differently. Do not be anxious for anything. Do not be full of care. Do not be full of worry. Do not be full of defeat. Do not be full of fear. Do not be troubled or upset. Instead, set your emotions on the things above.

> *Do not fret because of evil men*
> *or be envious of those who do wrong;*
> *for like the grass they will soon wither,*
> *like green plants they will soon die away.*
> *Trust in the LORD and do good;*
> *dwell in the land and enjoy safe pasture.*

Delight yourself in the LORD
and he will give you the desires of your heart.
(Psalm 37:1-4)

If it looks like someone else is getting the blessing of God and you are not, say no to the emotion
of jealousy. Instead, choose to rejoice for the other
person. When someone is doing negative things in
your life, that is the time for you to get into the Land
of Promise. It is there that you can feast off of God's
promises and faithfulness to you. If you allow yourself to be anxious, you will not experience the emotions that God wants you to that will bring you into
the life of God. The direction that your emotions go
is a choice that you make. You are responsible for
the behavior of your emotions, no one else.

I recall a day when I was young in the Lord
and we got some negative news. I was in the kitch-
en at the time and I could feel oppression come over
me. It was an instant sadness that I felt deep down.
I felt like the rug had been pulled out from under
me. My mind went completely blank and I couldn't
think of a single promise, not one good thing.

Rather than let that emotion control my life,
however, I chose to set my affections, my emotions,
on God and God said to me, "Jesus is Lord. Start
thanking me for Jesus."

I couldn't think of anything else. My mind
was totally blank and oppressed with the darkness

of negative news. So I set the timer for twenty minutes and began walking around saying, "Jesus. Thank you, Jesus. Thank you, Jesus." That was all I could think of to say.

But the important thing is that I made the choice to do it, in spite of how I felt, and in just twenty minutes, the oppression completely lifted and I stepped into the realm of God. My words lifted me into the realm of God's promises. Instead of going down, I went up to heaven. I embraced God's promises instead of the negative emotions. I entered into joy and I was in the realm of faith.

It is extremely important to take charge of your emotions before they ruin you. Emotions were given to us for a purpose, to help us build the kingdom of God, to build our lives and to build the lives of those around us. When we submit our emotions to the Holy Spirit by setting our affections on the things of God, they will connect us to the very life of God.

> *Those who live according to the sinful nature have their minds set on what that nature desires; but those who live in accordance with the Spirit have their minds set on what the Spirit desires.* (Romans 8:5)

Choose to set your emotions on the things that the Spirit desires. Choose to set your affections on life.

2
The Purpose of Emotions

The book of Job portrays a man leaning on his own righteousness and not the righteousness of God that would come from the Messiah. Job was under law and not grace. By his actions, he was saying, "I can do it myself. I don't need a redeemer." This attitude threw him into a life of fear that brought an unbelievable amount of disaster to him.

> *All who rely on observing the law are under a curse, for it is written: "Cursed is everyone who does not continue to do everything written in the Book of the Law."* (Galatians 3:10)

Satan is a legalist. God has bound Himself to His Word. So Job lived under the curse of trying to do it all himself. But by the end, he realized he needed a redeemer and he connected himself to the Word and then he was able to leave the law and connect to grace. Job received twice as much under grace. To get to that point, however, Job went through a time of disaster.

> *Then the LORD answered Job out of the*
> *whirlwind, and said:*
> *"Who is this who darkens counsel*
> *By words without knowledge?*
> *Now prepare yourself like a man;*
> *I will question you, and you shall answer*
> *Me.*
>
> (Job 38:1-3 NKJV)

Job lost virtually everything, including his children. It created intense emotions in him. He tore his robe and shaved his head in his grief (Job 1:20). He sat down and did not move for a long time. When he finally did speak, the emotion of grief overwhelmed him. His first words were to curse the day of his birth (Job 3:1).

As often happens to us when we are going through a difficult time, Job had friends that were more harm than good to him. They came and tried to console him but most of what they had to say was not very helpful. In fact, they were more judgmental than consoling. They accused him of not being spiritual.

> *But now trouble comes to you, and you are dis-*
> *couraged;*
> *it strikes you, and you are dismayed.*
> *Should not your piety be your confidence*
> *and your blameless ways your hope?*
> (Job 4:5-6)

It was God Himself to whom Job finally listened. He told Job to set his emotions on the things above. Through several chapters, God points out the things that Job should pay attention to. He reminds Job that it is God who made the world and the heavens and it is God who has them all under control. He got Job to stop looking at his own problem and the works of the devil and start looking at the things of God. He told him to act like a man and prepare himself by setting his emotions where they belonged. When Job did that, he began to see things God's way.

> *My ears had heard of you*
> *but now my eyes have seen you.*
> (Job 42:5)

The result was that Job came out of his grief and began to experience restoration. He moved into abundance and he lived in joy and peace. By setting his emotions in the Kingdom of God, he brought them under control and they brought him into life.

Connecting to Faith

God created emotions to bring good to us. Too often we have considered all emotions to be bad and we have become frustrated in trying to get rid of them. They just won't completely go away. That is because they are not supposed to go away. Rather, they are meant to be trained to accomplish what God intended and to bring the feeling of abundant life to us.

What good are emotions? Why did God give them to us? They are designed to bring us into the love of God. They are to bring us into His goodness and His kindness. They are to bring us into peace. They are to bring us into self-control. In short, emotions are to produce the fruit of the Spirit in our lives and to bring us into the passion of God so that we can be generous to give them to others—love goodness, kindness, peace and more. We can only give what we have.

Emotions are where you feel the life of God, where you sense His presence. Emotions create an atmosphere in which God can bring growth and life to us. That joy became my connector to faith when I was in crisis and that faith brought me into an awareness of God's presence. Emotions are given to us to bring us into faith.

> *Consider it pure joy, my brothers, whenever you face trials of many kinds, because you know that the testing of your faith develops perseverance. Perseverance must finish its work so that you may be mature and complete, not lacking anything. (James 1:2-4)*

God did not bring the trial. It is the devil who attacks you, not God. But when the trial comes, God will use it to produce good in you. James says to count it pure joy. It is not the trial you are re-joicing in but rather the Lord's promises that you have already won the battle and in Him you are already blessed. Another translation says, "Don't allow yourself to have any other emotions but joy." The reason you can do this is that you are not rejoic-ing over the trial but you are rejoicing because you have faith in Him and the promises of God in Christ. So you can embrace that and step into a winning attitude.

> Emotions are where you feel the life of God, where you sense His presence.

This is what happens when you start to count it all joy. Your subconscious, which doesn't know the difference between a good confession and re-ality, will say, "She's rejoicing, so she has already won. It's done." In that moment, you enter into pure faith and conceive the promise and it will be-come flesh and dwell among you.

If you don't rejoice, you will not get connected to faith and you will go under. It's as simple as that. Instead of living by faith, you are living by what you see. And that will cause you to lose out on so much that God wants for you. Choose joy instead and it will connect you to faith.

Emotions are given to us to enjoy. They bring us into passion. The Bible tells us that a tree of life grows in us when a desire is fulfilled.

Hope deferred makes the heart sick, but
when the desire is fulfilled, it is a tree of life.
(Proverbs 13:12 AMP)

The emotions of God bring life to us simply
because we enjoy them. They bring the very life
of God. There are so many emotions that we can
enjoy in our walk with God. The joy that comes
from His presence is one. The enjoyment of your
mate and your children, the pleasures of family, will
add to your life. The good emotions of belonging to
the family of God, the church, and the pleasure that
comes from finding and living your destiny are all
emotions that will bring the abundant life of God to
you. They will enable you to experience the love of
God, the goodness and the healing of God and all of
the great things that He has for you.

Emotional Self-Control

It is interesting that so many people think
that they cannot control their emotions. Yet God
commanded us to have certain emotions. He must
think that it is possible to change them by our decision to obey Him. He commanded us because He
created us in such a way that our emotions can be
a benefit to us if we bring them into submission to
the Holy Spirit.

Joshua could easily have given in to emotions of fear and anxiety as he considered the task

ahead of him. Still, he was commanded not to have negative emotions.

> *Have I not commanded you? Be strong and courageous. Do not be terrified; do not be discouraged, for the LORD your God will be with you wherever you go.* (Joshua 1:9)

Israel was about to go into battle and God said to trust in Him. The same principle holds true for us. God is saying that we are to enter the land that He has promised us, the land flowing with milk and honey, the land the devil has taken and is living in. We are going to take back the blessings he has stolen from us. We are going to get him off the land and out of our promises. We are going to possess the land. So God says, "Don't you dare be afraid. Don't you dare be discouraged. Don't you dare be dismayed." God has commanded you to choose the emotions of joy and courage and confidence because God has already won. You need to see that you have already won and you are victorious. Use your emotions to bring you into faith and into courage.

You have a responsibility before God with your emotions. The Bible says to serve the Lord with gladness. When Israel failed to do that, the result was that they fell. God warned them to control their emotions and to be glad.

*Because you did not serve the LORD
your God joyfully and gladly in the time of
prosperity, therefore in hunger and thirst,
in nakedness and dire poverty, you will
serve the enemies the LORD sends against
you.* (Deuteronomy 28:47-48)

The emotions of joy and gladness served to
connect Israel to prosperity and to freedom. God
has given us everything we need for a godly and
fulfilling life.

*His divine power has given us every-
thing we need for life and godliness through
our knowledge of him who called us by his
own glory and goodness. Through these he
has given us his very great and precious
promises, so that through them you may par-
ticipate in the divine nature and escape the
corruption in the world caused by evil desires.* (2 Peter 1:3-4)

Emotions help us experience the life of God.
Through them we can experience the very nature
of God. We become partakers of His divine nature.
No matter what the situation, we have the ability
to choose to live in the promises of God and they
will bring us victory in every circumstance. They
will make us more than conquerors. We will escape

the destruction caused by "evil desires," that is, by negative emotions. God intended that our emotions bring us life by bringing us into His nature.

It is absolutely vital to recognize that you can choose the emotions that you will live by. If you choose those that are negative, those that are connected to evil desires, then you will be choosing destruction. If you choose God's emotions, then you will connect to His joy, His peace, His confidence and His life. It really is a matter of choice.

This day I call heaven and earth as witnesses against you that I have set before you life and death, blessings and curses. Now choose life, so that you and your children may live and that you may love the LORD your God, listen to his voice, and hold fast to him. For the LORD is your life, and he will give you many years in the land he swore to give to your fathers, Abraham, Isaac and Jacob. (Deuteronomy 30:19-20)

3

Fortified Cities

Joshua faced a significant stronghold in his life. It was named Jericho and it was a fortified city. It was one of many that Israel found in the Promised Land. They all stood in the way of occupying the place God had promised them. There were many, and most of them were pretty strong. The spies that Moses sent in years earlier had been impressed by them, even afraid of them. They brought their report to Moses.

> *But the people who live there are powerful, and the cities are fortified and very large.* (Numbers 13:28)

The thought in their minds was one of defeat. They saw themselves as small and weak. They experienced the emotions of fear and intimidation and it made them believe that they couldn't succeed.

> *But the men who had gone up with him said, "We can't attack those people; they are stronger than we are." And they spread among the Israelites a bad report about the*

land they had explored. They said, "The land we explored devours those living in it. All the people we saw there are of great size. We saw the Nephilim there (the descendants of Anak come from the Nephilim). We seemed like grasshoppers in our own eyes, and we looked the same to them. (Numbers 13:31-33)

Joshua had been a part of that expedition. He and Caleb were the only two of the spies who did not have the thought of failure and weakness in their minds. Caleb spoke for both of them. They recognized that our thoughts produce our emotions. Joshua and Caleb had a different spirit because they embraced the thoughts of God and what God said. So, instead of the fear of the other ten spies, they had emotions of courage and faith and excitement in challenging the enemy.

Then Caleb silenced the people before Moses and said, "We should go up and take possession of the land, for we can certainly do it." (Numbers 13:30)

They were ready to take the land. If a stronghold stood in their way, they were ready to tear it down because their emotions were winning emotions and they had already won in their minds.

Jericho, however, was one of the most formidable strongholds in the land. It was the oldest city in the world and it had mud brick walls six and a half feet thick and fifteen feet high. It stood on a plain where it dominated the main route into Canaan from the east. If Joshua was going to take the land, he had to start with Jericho. There was no way around it.

But Joshua already believed he could take this fortified city. No other thought entered his mind. He looked to God for instructions, not about whether or not to proceed, but just the details of how. In his mind, the victory was already won.

Then the LORD said to Joshua, "See, I have delivered Jericho into your hands, along with its king and its fighting men. March around the city once with all the armed men. Do this for six days. Have seven priests carry trumpets of rams' horns in front of the ark. On the seventh day, march around the city seven times, with the priests blowing the trumpets. When you hear them sound a long blast on the trumpets, have all the people give a loud shout; then the wall of the city will collapse and the people will go up, every man straight in. (Joshua 6:2-5)

Where did Joshua and Caleb get the courage to press forward when so many others around them held back in fear? It began with a thought. The fear of the others began with the thought that they were grasshoppers. The courage of Joshua and Caleb began with the thought that they couldn't be beaten. Thoughts produce emotions. Emotions produce action.

Bringing Down Your Strongholds

The Old Testament is a picture of life in the New Testament. When we look at the fortified city of Jericho in the Old Testament, we see a picture of strongholds in our lives. There have been fortified cities in our minds that have controlled access to the Promised Land that God has planned for us. He promised us health and prosperity and peace. But to get there, we might have to go through the Jericho in our minds that tells us we can't win. We have to overcome the emotions of fear and intimidation and rejection.

We can see from the way Joshua attacked the city that he understood how to harness his emotions. He didn't agree with the other spies. He thought differently.

We can learn an important lesson, too, from the way Joshua approached the stronghold of Jericho. Six is a number that is used symbolically to represent man. Seven is the number of the Sabbath. For six days, Israel marched around the problem without getting in, much the way we go around and around some of our problems without ever getting rid of them.

The seventh day represented leaving behind man's way of doing things and entering into God's Sabbath rest. As we saw earlier, we are commanded to be anxious for nothing, to not let our hearts be troubled. That is what a

> It all depends on what thoughts you entertain.

Sabbath rest is all about. On the seventh day, they fulfilled Psalm 100. They gave a shout. And the result was complete victory.

The same principles are true today. A stronghold in your life is something that rises up in your mind and produces thoughts that are contrary to the Word of God. If you dwell on those thoughts, it will create emotions that will bring destruction in your life and prevent you from enjoying the promises of God. It all depends on what thoughts you entertain.

Every emotion is born out of a thought. When you get your thoughts under control, your emotions will come under control as well. When you direct your thoughts, you direct your emotions. You set your emotions on the things of God by controlling your thoughts. The battle is in your head and it is done with spiritual weapons.

For though we live in the world, we do not wage war as the world does. The weapons we fight with are not the weapons of the world. On the contrary, they have divine power to demolish strongholds. We demolish arguments and every pretension that sets itself up against the knowledge of God, and we take captive every thought to make it obedient to Christ. (2 Corinthians 10:3-5)

It is not by human strength that we wage war. It is a spiritual battle and we wage war with spiritual weapons. They are divine power to us. They are resurrection power in us.

That power will win the battle in your mind specifically by pulling down strongholds and destroying them, crumpling them and getting rid of them forever. That power will put them under your feet forever.

What are those strongholds? The Bible calls them arguments that set themselves up against the knowledge of God. They are the arguments that you hear in your head, that voice in your ear that tries to tell you that you can't win. The cities are too strong and the giants are too big.

If you allow those thoughts to continue, they will produce the emotions of fear, failure, discouragement, oppression and sadness and your actions will follow them. You have to tear down that stronghold by taking those thoughts captive and replacing them with thoughts that agree with the Word of God.

What does God say? Through His Word, He says that you have victory, that you have joy and favor and love, that you are made in His image. God says that you are brilliant because you have the mind of Christ. You are successful. You are wealthy. You are healthy. That is how God sees you. That is the knowledge of God and those strongholds are arguing against it.

Any argument that exalts itself against God will lead you to destructive

> That power will win the battle in your mind specifically by pulling down strongholds.

emotions if you let it remain. It is a roadblock to your Promised Land. It may not be a big thing, but often it is little things that slow us down.

I have to watch what I eat at times. I don't want to gain weight. God doesn't want me to gain weight, either, and my husband certainly doesn't want me to gain weight. It would not be healthy and it would have a negative effect on my life. I wouldn't look my best and I wouldn't feel my best. So I watch what I eat.

A couple of years ago, we were at a wedding in Hawaii. The son of one of my best friend's got married, so it was a special occasion. The first thing I saw as I walked outside was a huge spread of food and wonderful deserts and chocolate. Immediately my emotions started to say, "It's a special event. Live it up. It's a party tonight. Eat whatever you feel like. You need this time to relax and have fun."

I got up to the buffet, however, and I began to think about what I was about to do. I thought, let's talk about this. And I started talking to my emotions. "Do you want to do this? Do you want to pay the consequences of what's going to happen once I have this big celebration? Are you really thinking about how much this is going to cost me?" I told my emotions that we were not going to do that. "It's not worth it. I don't need to have to have all that food to have a good time."

Once I said that, the desire just died right there. I was excited about eating healthy food.

Emotions are very susceptible to influence. You have great power over them if you just take the time to actually talk to them and take charge of them. Declare the truth and bring your emotions out of the lie. If I had let my emotions dictate my behavior, they would have led me in a direction that I did not want to go. They would have been destructive. But we all have the power to bring emotions under control.

Thoughts and Emotions

No emotion stands alone. It always begins with a thought. To control emotions, we have to deal with the source. The Word tells us to take on the attitude of Christ Jesus. It is something that we need to do every day. Once we do that, once we adopt the right attitude, our thoughts will follow and once our thoughts are in line with the Word, our emotions will follow them. The ten spies had wrong thoughts, thoughts of weakness and defeat and the emotions of fear and discouragement followed them. Joshua and Caleb had thoughts of victory and strength and their emotions fell right in line.

We are what we think. Scripture bears that out.

For as he thinketh in his heart, so is he.
(Proverbs 23:7 KJV)

Your thoughts will create your emotions. Your emotions will dictate your behavior. They will dictate your emotional response to life. Where you place your emotions will depend on the thoughts that you have. If you allow yourself to think ugly and sad and negative thoughts, then your emotions will go to sadness, depression and grief. You will live in misery because of where you allow your thoughts to take your emotions.

If you choose to think other thoughts, however, your emotions will fall in line. If you do exactly what Psalm 100 says, then you will start the day by shouting for joy. You will wake up and speak gladness. You will think thoughts of joy and victory. It is so important that you realize it is in your power to do that. You can shout for joy even when you don't feel joyous. The feeling is an emotion and it will follow wherever you direct your thoughts. When you choose to speak joy, even though you don't feel it, you will not go very long before you do start to feel it. Your emotions will follow your thoughts. Shouting with the shout of gladness is obedience to God and that obedience will produce good emotions.

I tend to be a very task-oriented person. I begin each day by quoting God's Word, but I always have a list of things that I need to do. In the past I have always set out to do them without thinking about any kind of emotions. It's not that I am sad or depressed. I really don't feel any emotion. It is just a list of tasks and they need to be done. I do not even think about serving God with gladness, just about serving God.

But God showed me that I need to do everything with gladness. Each task that I accomplish, I need to do it with the emotion of gladness as unto the Lord. It doesn't matter what the task is. I am to do it with gladness as though it is directly in service to God, whether it is work, school, errands, work in the church or meeting the needs of my family. All of it is part of my service to God and I need to do it with gladness and joy. As God showed me that, I purposed to have that emotion. I chose to think thoughts of joy and gladness—and my emotions quickly followed.

You choose your thoughts. Your thoughts produce your emotions and your emotions produce your behavior. When you don't feel joy and you decide to think thoughts of joy and declare joy, you call that which is not as though it is and your gladness links you to faith. When faith is turned loose, your emotions will follow. Controlling your emotions means coming into agreement with God and with His Word. When you do that, you will become Spirit-led, not emotionally driven. When you set your mind or your affections on the things of God and how marvelous He is, it is impossible to be depressed. It is impossible to be miserable.

> You choose your thoughts. Your thoughts produce your emotions. and your emotions direct your behavior.

When I was young in the Lord, I didn't know all of this. There was no teaching available that talked about emotions. One day I woke up and I was in deep, extreme depression. I don't even really know why. It surrounded me and I felt like I was in complete darkness.

Tom would come home from work and ask how I was, hoping I would answer that I was okay. But I wasn't. Day after day, he would ask the same question and still the depression continued. A month later, it was still the same. There was nothing bad going on. It was just the result of negative thoughts.

I remember the day, however, that I woke up and said, "I'm going to call those things that are not as though they were." In spite of the fact that I felt depressed, I declared that it was the best day of my life. All day long I kept saying that. I kept telling myself, "You are so happy. You've never been happier."

My mind kept arguing with me. "Look at you. You're not happy. You feel depressed." I so wanted to admit that I was miserable inside. I so wanted to say that no one understood me or how much I was suffering.

But I kept at it. I saw it as a stronghold that needed to be torn down, a fortified city that was keeping me from my Promised Land, my destiny. I determined to cast those thoughts down and I said, "No, in the name of Jesus."

Tom was a youth pastor at the time. That night he left for the church and I stayed home to prepare a lesson. In the middle of that study, the power of God came over me and flooded me with joy. It broke that stronghold and the darkness and depression disappeared. I began crying for joy as I experienced the emotions that God wanted me to have. I remembered that the Word says, when I sit in darkness, He will be a light to me. The stronghold of depression fell when I determined that I was not going to think or say anything that was in agreement with the depression. Instead I would think and say only that which agreed with the Word of God. By my choice, I was able to break the depression off of me and enter into the joy of the Kingdom.

4

Thinking God's Thoughts

The Bible tells us that Jesus was "tempted in every way, just as we are—yet was without sin" (Hebrews 4:15). He even experienced the same kinds of emotional pressures that you and I do. But He always kept His emotions subject to the control of the Holy Spirit. He always directed His life according to the thoughts of the Father.

The night before His crucifixion, Jesus went to the Garden of Gethsemane to pray. While in prayer, His emotions welled up and He was in great anguish because of it.

> *He withdrew about a stone's throw beyond them, knelt down and prayed, "Father, if you are willing, take this cup from me; yet not my will, but yours be done." And angel from heaven appeared to him and strengthened him. And being in anguish, he prayed more earnestly, and his sweat was like drops of blood falling to the ground.* (Luke 22:41-44)

Jesus knew He was close to death and His emotions didn't like it. They screamed for some other solution. Jesus felt the emotions of the moment and they caused Him anguish.

He expressed His emotions to the Father, but He did not let them control Him. Instead, He sought the will of the Father and He brought His emotions into submission to God's thoughts. Jesus determined to obey God rather than His feelings. Thoughts will direct your emotions and Jesus sought the thoughts of God first.

The battle is in the mind. Will you think the thoughts that God has for you and dictate to your emotions where they are going to be placed or will you think the thoughts that your emotions dictate to you so that you are controlled by them? Jesus experienced the same conflict that you and I go through, but He overcame the emotions of the crisis and He chose the Father's will instead of His own. When Jesus chose to direct His thoughts toward the thoughts of God, notice that an angel came to strengthen Him. God is always ready to send the power that you need as soon as you direct your thoughts toward Him.

Capturing Your Thoughts

The fortified cities that we encounter are in our minds. They are the places that the enemy has been controlling by giving us thoughts that are against the knowledge of God, thoughts that argue against God and that exalt themselves above God. They produce emotions that cause destruction in your life—to your relationships, your marriage, your children and your work.

But you have within your grasp the power to tear down those strongholds. You can direct your thoughts toward the thoughts of God. You can shout for joy and bring those walls down.

You need to understand that it is not just a matter of thinking right. The world often says that you just need to think positive. Thinking positive is only a part of the process, however. You do need to think positive but you also need to have the resurrection power of the Holy Spirit at work that comes from our confession of God's Word. There is power in what you say.

The tongue has the power of life and death,
and those who love it will eat its fruit.
(Proverbs 18:21)

The power of the tongue is resurrection power. When God's Word is spoken out, the tongue has creative power. You have to realize you have the power to talk your emotions out of going crazy, doing the wrong thing, eating the wrong food, having unmanaged anger and being destructive. I call this the "Supernatural Power of Self-Talk."

You talk to your emotions. You harness them by talking sense into them. You have the power to bring them under the obedience of the

Holy Spirit. You can talk them out of road rage or overreacting to sports. You can say no to the victim role or you can talk them out of going into a fit in your marriage.

It isn't just positive thinking but it does require thinking positive. How much God can do in your life will be largely determined by how you think. If you learn to say "no" to wrong thoughts and "yes" to the thoughts of God, then your emotions will lead you toward faith and you will find the power of God unleashed on your behalf. The fortified cities will crumble before you.

It all starts with your thoughts. If your thoughts are not right, direct them through your confession. When your emotions controlled your thoughts, you always looked for the bad: "People are dumb. My job is awful. I hate my life. I hate my marriage. I hate my kids." When the Holy Spirit controls your thoughts, you will confess what God thinks about you instead: "I see the best in people. I am brilliant because I have the mind of Christ. I am the light of Jesus to those around me. I love my spouse. I love my children. I love my job. I will go to work early. I will work hard. I will be a blessing to everyone around me. I will bring favor to them and blessing to them. I will bring value to people." It all starts with how you think.

The Bible speaks at great length about the need to change how we think. Ephesians 4:23 calls it being "renewed in the spirit of your mind" (KJV). In the New International Version, it is the "attitude of your minds." You are to have new spiritual and mental attitudes in your life.

God has thoughts and He wants to reveal them to us.

However, as it is written:

"No eye has seen,
   no ear has heard,
no mind has conceived
   what God has prepared for those who love
      him"—

but God has revealed it to us by his Spirit. The Spirit searches all things, even the deep things of God. (1 Corinthians 2:9-10)

The mind cannot grasp or comprehend God's plans for us, but the Spirit of God will reveal it. God wants to captivate your mind and bring it into order. That is why He commands you to bring every thought into captivity. Another translation uses the word "grabbing" them and making them surrender to what God says. You set the course of your thoughts and the Holy Spirit will reveal to you God's thoughts for you. He is searching the deep things of God. We need the Holy Spirit if we are to know God's thoughts.

> *For who among men knows the thoughts of a man except the man's spirit within him? In the same way no one knows the thoughts of God except the Spirit of God.* (1 Corinthians 2:11)

It is the Holy Spirit who knows the thoughts of God toward us. He searches the deep things of God so that He can reveal them to us. He will bring those nuggets into our minds and say, "These are the thoughts you are to have." We receive the Holy Spirit precisely because He wants to reveal to us the thoughts of God.

> *We have not received the spirit of the world but the Spirit who is from God, that we may understand what God has freely given us.* (1 Corinthians 2:12)

The **NKJV** says the "things" God has given you. I have received the Holy Spirit because He wants to invade my mind in order to give me the thoughts of God. Once I come into agreement with those thoughts, my emotions will follow and I will be successful as I walk in His divine nature.

We can direct our thoughts through confession. As we speak out the thoughts that God gives us, our emotions come into line with them.

This is what we speak, not in words taught us by human wisdom but in words taught by the Spirit, expressing spiritual truths in spiritual words. (1 Corinthians 2:13)

Thoughts direct emotions. If it was just a matter of positive thinking, we would be in trouble. But God has sent the Holy Spirit to reveal to us the thoughts of God so that we can agree with them and set our emotions on the things of God. God has many thoughts toward you and they are all for good.

How precious to me are your thoughts, O God!
  How vast is the sum of them!
Were I to count them,
  they would outnumber the grains of sand.
                    (Psalm 139:17-18)

Another Psalm speaks of how great and uncountable God's thoughts are toward us:

Many, O LORD *my God, are Your wonderful*
  works
Which You have done;
And Your thoughts toward us
Cannot be recounted to You in order;
If I would declare and speak of them,
they are more than can be numbered.
                    (Psalm 40:5 NKJV)

By tapping into God's thoughts, you can have complete victory over those fortified cities that have plagued you in the past. When those thoughts that are opposed to the knowledge of God rise up in your mind and try to bring you into destructive emotions, you can look to the Holy Spirit to bring your thoughts into agreement with the knowledge of God. Set your affections on the things of God and you will be Spirit-led, not emotionally-driven.

A New Attitude

Ephesians 4:23 calls it a new attitude of your mind. An attitude involves a certain determination. The attitude that God wants you to have is that you are going to love life. You are going to be excited. You are full of joy. You must be determined to take on this attitude and connect to the thoughts of God and thus bring your emotions into submission. Your attitude will then change your thoughts and your thoughts will change your emotions and your emotions will change your behavior.

The apostle Paul spoke openly about his failures. In Romans 7, he described his inability to do the things he wanted to do and to stop doing the things he did not want to do. He blamed it on the sin that lived in him.

Now if I do what I do not want to do, it is no longer I who do it, but it is sin living in me that does it. (Romans 7:20)

Paul recognized the stronghold that needed to be eliminated. The fortified city was sin that lived in him and he had no control over it.

> *What a wretched man I am! Who will rescue me from this body of death?* (Romans 7:24)

But he has the answer immediately.

> *Thanks be to God—through Jesus Christ our Lord!* (Romans 7:25)

In chapter 8, Paul begins to describe the law of the Spirit. It is in verse 4 that he gives an important clue to entering into freedom. It requires that we no longer live according to the sinful nature but rather according to the Spirit.

> The sinful nature lives according to destructive emotions.

The sinful nature lives according to destructive emotions—whatever feels good at the moment. It produces the emotions of self. People who live in self will find their emotions leading them into adultery, jealousy, murder, gossip and all kinds of destructive things. It all comes back to where your thoughts are set.

Those who live according to the sinful nature have their minds set on what that nature desires; but those who live in accordance with the Spirit have their minds set on what the Spirit desires. (Romans 8:5)

Those who live according to the Spirit have set their minds, their thoughts, their affections on the things of God. They have connected to what the Holy Spirit wants, not what the flesh desires.

Of course, that means that you have to die to self. Jesus said that he who loses his life will gain it (Luke 17:33). When you choose to die to your own desires and set your thoughts on God, he will bring good things to you and you will experience life. If you do not, your emotions will lead you and bring destruction.

The mind of sinful man is death, but the mind controlled by the Spirit is life and peace. (Romans 8:6)

When I was about thirty I was actively involved in the women's ministry called Aglow. I loved it and I loved the girls that I worked with. I had my own chapter and I saw great success. I traveled and had a wonderful time. I was so excited about that ministry that I thought the next step would be to get on the area board and I so wanted to be on area board.

But God had other things in mind for me. He said, "I want you to build a children's church."

I didn't want to do that. But it was God's will and I couldn't do both. I had small children. If I was going to obey God, then I would have to give up my activities with Aglow. I had one desire, but I had to set my mind on God's will, not my own. So I had to say no to my will and embrace the will of God. I set my mind on what the Holy Spirit desired and I served with gladness in the children's church.

> When you choose to die to your own desires and set your thoughts on God, He will bring good things to you.

Instead of losing out on what I gave up, the children's church became such a blessing. I was able to be the children's church pastor for my own boys and be a direct part of their lives, building those memories with them. God knew exactly what was most important to me at that time in my life.

There have been many other times that I wanted to do one thing but God had something else in mind. In every case, once I died to self and brought my thoughts and emotions into submission to the Holy Spirit, what God wanted was also the most exciting and the most fulfilling for me.

Before we started the church, I loved traveling. I had a great passion for speaking to congregations all over the country. We had just been to

Chicago where we had appeared on television. I had been traveling for a week by myself, speaking in different churches, and Tom joined me for another week. We were on our way home and, as we sat together on the plane, I was so excited that I was high. I told Tom, "I absolutely love this traveling."

We got home and found out that God called us to build a church. That wasn't what I wanted to do. I wanted to travel. But I had to die to myself and set my mind on the thoughts of God for me. When the church first started, I prayed day and night and believed God. Then Aglow or some other church would call and want me to speak, so I still traveled.

One day God said to me, "You're going to have to decide what you're going to do. You can either travel or you can build a church. You're going to have to decide. But I called you to build a church."

That was it. I was done traveling at that time. At the beginning of the church, it was like a baby being birthed and it required my full focus and attention. I couldn't do that and travel. So I had to say, "Not my will, but yours be done."

From that time, when I got calls to speak, I had to say no to them. I can't travel right now. But that's okay. I'm excited about what God has called me to do. I set my thoughts on the call of God in my life and now, years later, I do some traveling.

Today, building the church is the passion of my life. I absolutely love it. My emotions came into line with the Holy Spirit as I died to self and set my affections on the things of God. I absolutely love what I do.

Setting your mind on God is a way of declaring that you know what God wants is also what is best for you. It might seem painful at the beginning, but there is no greater joy than to be right where God wants you. It will always be for your good.

You must develop the right attitude. Your attitude will direct your thoughts and your thoughts will direct your emotions. When you set your mind on God. You will live in peace.

You will keep him in perfect peace,
Whose mind is stayed on You,
Because he trusts in You.
(Isaiah **26:3 NKJV**)

5
Self-Talk

Over the years, my husband, Tom, has been intensely interested in nutrition. He has read dozens of books and studied the subject until he is now something of an expert. Of course, that means that he did not like it when I drank too much coffee, which I used to do. Tom told our kids that I was drinking poison. He didn't drink coffee and he didn't want them to, either.

Around that time I went through a serious illness that ended when God miraculously healed me. I was at lunch one day with my youngest son, Jason, and, with tears in his eyes, he said, "Mom, I'm praying that you will just quit drinking coffee." He was concerned that it would bring the sickness back.

Of course, as a mom, I wanted to see my son's prayers answered, so I said, "I'm done. I'll never drink coffee again."

It took three years to get free of the desire for coffee. Every time we were on a trip somewhere or when I would wake up in the morning, I had a great desire for coffee.

But I kept my word. I had promised my son and I had promised God. I did not have the coffee, but it made me so mad that I ever made the promise in the first place.

Ultimately, it was the power of the words I spoke that enabled me to get free of that desire. Every time the emotion would rise up in me and try to tell me that I really needed coffee, I talked to myself. I reminded myself of the promise I had made. I found that self-talk was a valuable tool in keeping my emotions under control.

Your emotions are stronger than your will, but they can be tamed and brought under control. You set your affections on the things of God. You direct your thoughts toward the thoughts of God, and your emotions will follow. When your emotions are under control, your behavior will no longer be destructive. Rather, it will become life-giving and positive.

You have to take charge of your emotions. You can't let them be in charge of you. You can make the choice. Your circumstances are not to choose how you feel; you are to choose. You must make a decision.

Recently, a friend of my son, Scot, asked him to have lunch with a friend of his. Scot agreed and when they met, he asked the man where he wanted to go. He said he didn't care, so Scot said, "Why don't you tell me what kind of food you like and I'll pick a restaurant?"

The man still said he didn't care, so Scot suggested a popular seafood restaurant. They went there and sat down for lunch. The man ordered a hamburger, so Scot said to him, "You know, they have really good fish here. Why don't you try some?"

"I don't like seafood," the man responded.

Scot asked him why he didn't say that before they got to the restaurant. They would have gone somewhere else. The man said he didn't want to be any trouble.

Then things got worse. When the hamburger arrived, it wasn't actually a hamburger at all. It was a kind of fish burger. Scot started to call the waiter over to fix it or get something else, but the man said, "No, no, I don't want to cause any hassle."

So the fish burger stayed. They finished lunch and left.

Some time later, the friend who originally asked Scot to have lunch with the man, contacted Scot and commented on what a horrible lunch it was. His friend was upset because he didn't like seafood and Scot took him to a seafood restaurant.

> You direct your thoughts toward the thoughts of God, and your emotions will follow.

Scot tried to explain what happened but the problem was simply that the man would not make a decision. Scot gave him several opportunities but he just didn't care. Because he wouldn't decide, he set his emotions up for a train wreck.

From that point on, it was the circumstances that determined his emotions.

If you do not make a decision and place your emotions where they belong, then you will be a victim to whatever circumstances bring you. You must decide.

If you do not, the emotions will bring destruction into your life. Sin is born out of uncontrolled emotions. The devil wants people to be emotionally-driven so that he can get them into sin and bring destruction to them.

Everyone meets with some adversity in life. That does not have to dictate what your emotions will be, however. There is a woman we see frequently at a local theatre. She is missing one leg and is confined to a wheel chair. But she is always happy. She loves life. She believes that every day is great. It is a decision that she makes to set her emotions in that realm. It doesn't matter what her circumstances are. She has chosen to be happy.

Your attitude in life will determine your thoughts in life. If you have the attitude that life is exciting and that you are thrilled with what God has called you to do, then your thoughts will follow. Your thoughts will determine your emotions. No emotion is on its own. Every emotion is created out of a thought.

Getting a Strategy

The next step that we need to deal with, then, is how to do all of this. How do you get the right emotions going on in your life?

First of all, you need to have a strategy. You need to think ahead in those areas where you have emotional weaknesses. There are certain circumstances that you know have always triggered wrong emotions in the past. Something happens and it always pushes you over the edge or there might be some desire that you've chased after that is not of God.

You need to make a plan before you are in that circumstance. How are you going to act? What will you do to handle the situation? Be proactive with your emotions. You have chosen to serve the Lord with gladness. Now, consider potential problems and situations that have caused you trouble in the past and decide now how you will react the next time. Have a plan.

This is where you can consider the power of your words. You talk to yourself. I learned the power of self-talk early in our marriage. I was always very easy going. I just flowed with everything, calm and good-natured. I got along with everyone.

When I started dating Tom, however, I found that he could push my buttons like nobody else could. We would get in the car to go somewhere and in five minutes I lost it emotionally. He would say something and it would make me so mad. We got married and it got even worse.

Then God began to show me that I could use the power of my words to bring those emotions under control. I started talking to myself, asking myself questions. "Is this really worth getting upset about? Is it worth all the energy that it is going to take to get mad? Is it worth what's going to happen today? Is it worth the consequences?"

All of a sudden those emotions began to settle down and come back into order. Then I could ask myself why that upset me so much and deal with whatever problem was there.

The next time the same situation came up, I was more ready to talk to my emotions and harness them before they ran wild and one day, I just wasn't reacting the same way anymore.

I mentioned earlier that I spent time working as a nurse. One of the things that we learned as part of that training was that the will is not as powerful as the emotions. If a person is an alcoholic, he might will to never drink again, but as soon as the desire begins to affect him, the emotions kick in and he can taste the drink and before long, he is drinking again. A drug addict might vow to never touch the drug again, but as soon as the desire happens, the emotion takes over and he begins to feel the effects of the drug. Before long, he is right back in it.

But the Bible tells us that the power of life and death is in the tongue (Proverbs 18:21). God spoke creation into existence. He said "Let there be light," and there was light. He has given us the very same power in our words to create control over our emotions and bring them back into submission to the Holy Spirit.

> The Bible tells us that the power of life and death is in the tongue.

Alcoholics need to get free of the power of that addiction, but if they will stop and begin to talk to themselves, they will find the tongue to be a powerful weapon that will enable them to take control of the emotions that lead them into the addiction in the first place. When the desire comes, they need to say to themselves, "You know, if you go out and get drunk tonight, you know you're going to come home and beat your wife and your kids. You're going to lose everything and you're not going to have enough money to pay your bills." As they begin to speak to themselves about the consequences of what will happen if they continue down that path, they can talk themselves right out of it.

If this is true in something as serious as alcohol and drug addiction, it is also true in every situation that you could find yourself in. In sports, we see emotions out of control all the time. We have seen basketball players run into the stands and start beating the fans just because a drink was thrown at them. We've seen baseball players throwing chairs at fans. We've seen fans attacking players. The results have been lawsuits and prosecutions for assault and, in some cases, the termination of great careers, all because they did not bring their emotions under control. In some cases, fans have been known to commit suicide because their favorite team did not win a championship game. Many go into great depression. Even those fans whose teams might win a national title will often go on a destructive rampage as they celebrate, turning over cars and smashing windows. The result is arrest and jail time, if not physical injury.

If you are a sports fan, then how can you prevent that kind of incident in your own life? Whether it is a matter of playing tennis or golf or going to a game, if you know from past experience that you have a problem keeping your emotions under control, you need to plan ahead. You need to start talking to yourself. You need to determine beforehand what you are going to say when you experience anger or depression because of the circumstances of the game. You need to be prepared to remind yourself that it is a game and it is not that big a deal. You need to be ready to tell yourself about the consequences of losing control of your emotions.

If you are in traffic and someone cuts you off and you know that you usually lose your temper, you need to plan ahead of time what you can do differently. How can you react in a way that would be better. Then you need to talk to yourself in the situation. Tell yourself that they might have a very good reason for being in such a hurry. Maybe they are in an emergency. Maybe they're late for work. Maybe they have something going on in their lives that is bringing them great stress and you need to bless them rather than curse them.

> If you have a plan, then you can practice self-talk and remind yourself of the plan.

You can plan how you will react to a traffic jam if that is something that usually brings you negative emotions. Tell yourself, "All right, I'm going to be in a traffic jam. Emotions, what are we going to do?" I can use the time to quote the Word. I can pray. I can get audio books or CDs of good preaching and spend the time listening to material that will improve my mind and spirit. If you have a plan, you can keep your emotions under control.

It might be your kids who trigger loss of control. Perhaps when you get involved in some project and your attention is focused and intense and the kids come barging in and interrupt you, you have always reacted badly. Maybe your husband or wife says or does something that always pushes you over the edge. You need a strategy ahead of time so that you are ready for the situation. It may be as simple as asking your kids if it is an emergency and, if it is not, ask them to give you thirty minutes and then you will talk to them. You need to talk to yourself and remind yourself of the consequences of a harsh reaction to your family.

The Power of Your Words

You need to have a plan. You must be able to stop before you react, grab those emotions and begin to talk to them and harness them. If you have a plan, then you can practice self-talk and remind yourself of the plan and of the right way to react in whatever situation you find yourself. Plan ahead and speak to yourself. The power of your words is tremendous.

> *For we all stumble in many things. If anyone does not sumble in word, he is a perfect man, able also to bridle the whole body.* (James 3:2 NKJV)

A perfect man is one who is emotionally mature. He is a grown-up. What the Word of God says here is that, in those moments when you feel your emotions trying to take control, when you are faced with a desire to do a wrong thing, to fall into a generational curse of alcohol or drugs, or a lust for adultery or pornography, any of those things that are wrong in God's eyes, you can be a mature person if you only will say the right thing. Bridle your tongue and direct what it says and it will set your thoughts in the right place, which will set your emotions in the right place, where God wants them, and your behavior will change. You will become emotionally mature.

The next verse elaborates on the amount of control the tongue has.

> *Look also at ships: although they are so large and are driven by fierce winds, they are turned by a very small rudder wherever the pilot desires. Even so the tongue is a little member and boasts great things. See how great a forest a little fire kindles!* (James 3:4-5 NKJV)

A ship is very large, yet it is controlled by a very small rudder. The tongue is small but it can control your thoughts and your emotions. If I may paraphrase James in the context of emotions, it will sound like this:

> *Although your emotions are large and are driven by fierce circumstances, you can turn your emotions around by what you say and change direction. Emotions will violate your will but your words will bring your emotions back into order to do what God wants and your emotions will then be able to fulfill*

God's purpose in your life. You can't control the wind or the sea, but you can set the sail for the direction you want to go and your sail is your tongue.

You can set your words. You can say the right things to go in the direction that you need to go. By learning self-talk, you can use your tongue to set boundaries to your emotions.

The Bible tells us to set our affections on the things of God. That begins by controlling your tongue. Set your speech and it will direct your thoughts and emotions. God wants you to set your emotions in the areas of joy, of gladness, of love and peace. He wants you to set your emotions in the areas of goodness and kindness and self-control. You have the power to choose that by choosing what your tongue says, regardless of the circumstances.

6
Setbacks

We love to hear rags to riches stories. It is so inspiring when someone overcomes all the odds and succeeds when everything was against them. Unfortunately, when it is you or me that is faced with opposition, it is much more difficult to stand up to it. For some reason we seem to think that if God wants us to have something, then it should come without any problem and we shouldn't have to do anything to get it. It should just happen while we relax and enjoy the blessing.

Of course, real life is not like that and when things don't go easily, we tend to start wondering why God is mad at us. The truth is that anything worth doing will probably meet with some resistance, from the devil if nothing else. It is because it is worth doing that we should persevere. The blessings are more than worth it when we are living in the Kingdom of God.

The great men of God in the Bible all had setbacks. There were always things that stood in the way of their destiny, but those who are remembered for overcoming did so by setting their affections on the things of God in spite of the obstacles before them.

If anyone ever had cause to give up, to throw in the towel and just quit, it would be David. He experienced major calamity in his life, even though he had a word from God. Nothing seemed to support that word. Every circumstance seemed to be against him from the beginning, yet he chose to remain joyful. He put into practice exactly what James later wrote about.

> *Consider it pure joy, my brothers, whenever you face trials of many kinds, because you know that the testing of your faith develops perseverance.* (James 1:2-3)

God started David out with pretty big news: he was going to be the king of Israel. That is quite a destiny to have presented to you at a young age.

From the very beginning, however, even his own family tried to leave him out. Samuel the prophet contacted David's father, Jesse and said, "I'm coming to your house." That was no small thing. Samuel was a celebrity, the spiritual leader of Israel at that time. It was like having Kenneth Copeland come to your home. Naturally the whole household got excited. They cleaned and dressed in their best clothes and made sure everything was perfect.

But David wasn't invited. They sent him out to take care of the sheep. He undoubtedly felt rejected and probably was devastated. Samuel came to anoint a king, but David's own father could not see him as a king, as a winner. Instead, he saw David as a failure, no better than a hired hand to water the sheep while more important people took care of more important things. David had to face the disappointment of his father's rejection.

But God saw David as king and that was what mattered. So David was anointed as king in spite of being left out. God did not overlook him. His family failed to include him, but God found him and anointed him anyway.

David may have thought that such recognition, being recognized as the next king of Israel, would have eliminated any other problems by bringing him acclaim and acceptance. But the next time we see David, he is back tending the sheep again. Here he is, the new king of Israel, and his family still has him doing menial labor.

But David kept the right attitude. He took that time to write music, to worship God, to develop his spiritual man and his relationship with God, and to prepare for the day when the vision would come to pass. David did not get discouraged. Many of the uplifting and encouraging Psalms came from that time in his life.

Inevitably the time came for David to be elevated. God began to promote him in the eyes of others. But that brought more problems—and it was still his family that was the worst.

Israel was at war with the Philistines and David's father sent him to the army's camp to take food to his brothers who were fighting with King Saul. At the time, the Philistine giant, Goliath, came out every day and challenged the Israelites. David was angered that no one stood up to him. He asked why none of the warriors accepted the challenge.

His oldest brother responded in anger.

> *When Eliab, David's oldest brother, heard him speaking with the men, he burned with anger at him and asked, "Why have you come down here? And with whom did you leave those few sheep in the desert? I know how conceited you are and how wicked your heart is; you came down only to watch the battle.* (1 Samuel 17:28)

This was the same David that God later said was a man after His own heart. But David's own family rejected him.

Still, God gave David favor with Saul and, after David killed Goliath, he married Saul's daughter, Michal. He sat at the king's table. Life for David appeared to be good at that point. He seemed to have the love, acceptance and favor of his father-in-law, King Saul and he seemed to be in the best possible position to succeed Saul as king. It looked like the word from God would certainly come to pass without any more problems.

That hope did not last long. Saul got jealous of David's popularity. All of Israel loved David, so

Saul tried to kill him and David had to run for his life. He lost his position. He lost his favor. He lost his wife. He lost everything. For three years David lived in the desert in caves or lived in exile in foreign countries that considered him an enemy.

In the midst of all of this, David chose to set his emotions on the things of God. He wrote Psalm 34 during that time of exile, while everything looked as bleak as it could get.

> *I will extol the LORD at all times;*
> *his praise will always be on my lips.*
> *My soul will boast in the LORD;*
> *let the afflicted hear and rejoice.*
> *Glorify the LORD with me;*
> *let us exalt his name together.*
> (Psalm 34:1-3)

David made a decision. Even though he had nothing and circumstances were against him, he decided that he would not be a victim. He would not be a wimp. He would not whine and complain and cry, "Why me?"

Instead, he set his emotions where they belonged—on the things of God. He determined to shout for joy and serve God with gladness. He harnessed his emotions and directed them. He controlled how he felt, not the circumstances around him.

Keeping Your Focus

No matter how much we plan, things don't always go the way we want them to. It is something that happens to everyone and it creates emotions such as frustration, anger and rejection. It can also make you want to just give up. That is when you need to get control of your emotions and deal with them before they rob you of your destiny and the promises of God.

The disappointment created by setbacks can easily cause you to focus on things that are not important to your destiny and ignore things that are. There was a time in my life when we were just beginning to come out of poverty and really experience the blessings that come through faith. We were going to get a particular house.

I was young in the Lord and this house I was believing for became an idol in my life. We drove by that house every night and confessed that it was ours. We expected that miracle. We planned to sell our current house so I hauled out signs and did an open house. I did everything there was to do. I was emotionally-driven concerning that house, not Spirit-led.

And then it didn't happen. We didn't get the house. We didn't experience the miracle. It seems like such a small thing today but at the time it was a major setback. Still, I had to harness those emotions. I realized that I needed to look at the bigger picture.

I remember talking to God as I drove home crying. I told God that seeing people saved was more important than a house. I said, "Lord, from now on, my faith is for salvation and for things that really matter in the kingdom. You will give me the house."

That was a major turning point in my life. I walked away from being possessed by things, from things having power over my emotions, and placed my desires and my emotions on the things of God. I have since been blessed with some wonderful things, including beautiful houses, but if I didn't have them tomorrow, it wouldn't matter. They have no power over me.

> A setback is easy to overcome when you set your affections on the things of God.

I realize in the scope of life, not getting a house was a small setback. But even with huge setbacks, we must learn how to emotionally handle them so that they don't control the rest of our lives. A setback is easy to overcome when you set your affections on the things of God.

You cannot take all of your faith and pour it into believing God that you'll never have another problem again. If you do, you can expect disappointment. God has given people free will and there will always be those who choose to embrace the desires of the flesh. Those people will always have conflict in life and they will create difficulties that will affect you. Other people will engage in wrong behavior. What others do or say is not in your control. But you can control how you react to it. You can set boundaries that will prevent other people's behavior from taking you into negative emotions and causing destruction in your life.

Jesus certainly confronted wrong behavior. He did not allow people to control His life. He demanded right behavior toward Himself. He also taught the disciples how to deal with rejection. Push it away.

> *If anyone will not welcome you or listen to your words, shake the dust off your feet when you leave that home or town.* (Matthew 10:14)

Obviously, I'm not saying to kick negative people out of your life. But shake the rejection off. Never let rejection stick to you. Rejection is a poison to your emotions and will make you emotionally ill. Rejection demands that you perform to be loved. Rejection will always put you in fear of not being loved unless you are perfect. Healthy love is unconditional love. You are loved because you exist, not because of what you do.

Just like brushing the dust off your feet, you can push away the rejection emotions that others want to inflict on you. You can walk away from it and leave nothing of yourself there. Don't even leave your peace. Never allow other people to control your emotions any more than you allow circumstances to have power over your emotions.

Circumstances will never determine happiness. If they did, movie stars would be the happiest people in the world. They have everything—success, money, big houses and expensive cars, to say nothing of popularity and friends—yet they are often the most miserable people you will ever meet. They are frequently on drugs or alcohol. Many are suicidal. Circumstances do not make you happy. Rather, happiness always comes from within. The Bible makes it clear that you can choose happiness in spite of setbacks.

> *Though the fig tree does not bud*
> *and there are no grapes on the vines,*
> *though the olive crop fails*
> *and the fields produce no food.*
> *though there are no sheep in the pen*
> *and no cattle in the stalls,*
> *yet I will rejoice in the* LORD,
> *I will be joyful in God my Savior.*
> (Habakkuk 3:17-18)

This is to be your attitude of life. It is the way to become mature and walk in the Kingdom of God. In the face of a setback, choose to rejoice. Even though you might lose everything, remember that when you have God, you have everything.

With that kind of attitude, you will be willing to take a risk and you will not go under if things go wrong. Setbacks do not bring an end to your life or your dreams. You will overcome.

It is possible to completely connect your emotions to your spirit, to hear from God and get the right emotional response in a negative situation. You have to learn from God how to develop healthy emotions that work with you and not against you. It is a choice that you make. It is a choice to be Spirit-led, not emotionally-driven.

The Apostle Paul

Paul is another example of a man of God who had to deal with setbacks. He had a clear direction from God. Jesus spoke to him on the road to Damascus and completely changed the direction of his life. Through Ananias, God gave him a wonderful vision for his ministry and his life.

> *But the Lord said to Ananias, "Go! This man is my chosen instrument to carry my name before the Gentiles and their kings and before the people of Israel. (Acts 9:15)*

That great goal in life also meant running into much opposition. People did not always embrace the gospel message joyfully. In Lystra, Paul was stoned and dragged outside the city where he was left for dead. Can you imagine what Paul endured? He was doing the work of God. He could have easily gotten mad at God for letting him be treated that way.

Instead, Paul set his emotions on the Kingdom of God. He got up and went back into the city (Acts 14:19-20). He could have taken the opportunity to run, but he chose to focus on the victory instead.

In Philippi, Paul cast a demon out of a slave girl. Instead of thanking him, her owners started a riot and Paul got arrested, beaten and thrown in jail. How did he react to this setback? He began singing (Acts 16:25).

Paul set his emotions on the work of God. After he began to worship, God sent an earthquake that opened the jail and knocked everyone's chains loose. Instead of running in fear while he had the chance, Paul started preaching the gospel to the other prisoners and then to the guards.

On another occasion, Paul was shipwrecked. He spent a day and a night in the water. He finally got to shore on the island of Malta, cold and wet. As if all of that wasn't enough, when he reached for some wood to put on the fire, a snake bit him. It made the superstitious people of the island turn away from him.

> *When the islanders saw the snake hang-*
> *ing from his hand, they said to each other,*
> *"This man must be a murderer; for though he*
> *escaped from the sea, Justice has not allowed*
> *him to live."* (Acts 28:4)

However, Paul just shook the snake off and the poison had no effect on him. God validated him because Paul chose to set his emotions on God instead of the circumstances. Paul died to himself and kept his emotions in the Kingdom of God.

Paul had plenty of setbacks in his life. He spoke openly about them.

> *Five times I received from the Jews the forty*
> *lashes minus one. Three times I was beaten with*
> *rods, once I was stoned, three times I was ship-*
> *wrecked, I spent a night and a day in the open*
> *sea, I have been constantly on the move. I have*
> *been in danger from rivers, in danger from ban-*
> *dits, in danger from my own countrymen, in dan-*
> *ger from Gentiles; in danger in the city, in danger*
> *in the country, in danger at sea; and in danger*
> *from false brothers. I have labored and toiled*
> *and have often gone without sleep; I have known*
> *hunger and thirst and have often gone without*
> *food; I have been cold and naked. Besides every-*
> *thing else, I face daily the pressure of my concern*
> *for all the churches.* (2 Corinthians 11:24-28)

In spite of all that, Paul never lost sight of the victory. He chose to rejoice and to sing. He chose to serve the Lord with gladness. He had a clear vision of eternity that enabled him to call those setbacks "light and momentary troubles."

> *Therefore we do not lose heart. Though outwardly we are wasting away, yet inwardly we are being renewed day by day. For our light and momentary troubles are achieving for us an eternal glory that far outweighs them all. So we fix our eyes not on what is seen, but on what is unseen. For what is seen is temporary, but what is unseen is eternal.* (2 Corinthians 4:16-18)

Paul considered the challenges in his life to be nothing more than bumps in the road, light afflictions. When you set your emotions on the things of God, when you die to yourself, even snake bites and shipwrecks become small things.

The glory that Paul said his afflictions were achieving means a manifestation of the power of God—the unceasing, never-ending blessings that follow us through all of eternity. That's what Paul got his eyes on. That's where he placed his emotions.

Pursuing the Prize

Even though you may run into obstacles as you set out to run your race, like David and Paul, you must keep your eyes on the outcome. You must keep the victory in mind. You are a winner, no matter what the enemy throws your way. In Jesus, you have won the battle and so you can rejoice. You can sing praises to God in the midst of the battle. You can see earthquakes happen for your benefit because you chose to link your emotions to joy and your joy linked you to faith and to the word of God.

You have to make a deliberate decision that you are not going to allow negative situations to mold your emotions or to determine your destiny. Begin to see obstacles as nothing more than little bumps in the road. That is how David and Paul looked at life and that is why they were successful. You can do the same.

I received an e-mail from a little girl in Iran. She was Islamic but she began to read the Bible and became a Christian and got connected with some Christian friends. All she wanted to do was to read the Bible.

One day the police came to her house, took her to prison and beat her repeatedly because she would not give up her faith in Jesus. When she got out of prison, she still read her Bible and confessed Jesus as her Lord. So the police came again. This time they beat her so badly that she ended up in the hospital.

At that point, she left the country. She is in Austria right now and wanted to tell me what was happening in her life and ask for prayer.

When I look at what that little girl has gone through, it seems like a sad comparison with how most Christians in America act. When the slightest thing goes wrong, we fall apart. We have not had to run for our lives. We have not been thrown in prison and beaten. Yet we see the most trivial things as a crisis.

We must begin to see our setbacks for what they are—little bumps in the road to our destiny. We need a new attitude. If you think something coming your way is a big deal, then it will be a big deal. But if your attitude sees it as a bump, it won't even slow you down. You won't miss a beat.

> Put your faith and your emotions in the eternal realm so that you can see the eternal picture.

Every day needs to be a celebration. Put your faith and your emotions in the eternal realm so that you can see the eternal picture. You need to develop a vision for eternity and an understanding that life here is only a vapor. You need to get it built into you so that your emotions don't go crazy every time something happens. We've been living in this life as though it's the only life we're ever going to live. We have to start looking into the eternal realm and see the glory, the manifestation of God's power and blessing.

Do not let your heart be troubled—no matter what happens around you. Push away anxiety. Do not be anxious for anything. God tells us to set our affections on His plans and His purposes. Paul constantly pushed toward the goals that God set before him. He never let himself get stuck in the negative emotions of setbacks.

> *Brethren, I do not count myself to have apprehended; but one thing I do, forgetting those things which are behind and reaching forward to those things which are ahead, I press toward the goal for the prize of the upward call of God in Christ Jesus.* (Philippians 3:13-14 NKJV)

Setbacks happen to everyone. But you don't have to get stuck in them. You don't have to embrace them. You might be victimized from time to time but you don't have to be a victim. Just like Paul shook the snake off of his arm, you can shake the setback off and move on in joy and in victory. It's no big deal. Just a bump in the road.

7
Conception in the Emotions

Emotions are inevitable. They are a part of what makes us who we are. Everyone feels them every day. We cannot escape from that. But that does not mean that emotions are bad. It is a matter of how and where we direct them.

It is also true that emotions conceive. If your emotions have been set on the things of God, they will conceive and give birth to a passion for the things of God. If your emotions are set on the desires of the flesh, they will conceive and give birth to sin. James talks about how sin is conceived in emotions.

> *When tempted, no one should say, "God is tempting me." For God cannot be tempted by evil, nor does he tempt anyone; but each one is tempted when, by his own evil desire, he is dragged away and enticed. Then, after desire has conceived, it gives birth to sin; and sin, when it is full-grown, gives birth to death.* (James 1:13-15)

When you don't take charge of your emotions and just let circumstances run them instead of you, then sin is going to happen in your life. Too often we blame God for things that go wrong in our lives, but God is only interested in doing good for you. He doesn't bring temptation and He doesn't bring destruction or sickness to you. It is not God who wants to hurt you. The devil is the one who wants you to suffer.

Temptation comes as a result of your own desires that produce emotions that are not harnessed and placed on the things of God. It comes from wrong desires, self-centered desires that we have not yet crucified. We have not gotten rid of them and they draw us away and entice us.

The word "entice" means that the enemy has put bait out there to capture you. If you don't make a decision to set your affections on the things of God, you will follow that enticement right into sin. For example, if you do not willfully decide to stay away from pornography, then whenever you feel that desire, you will be drawn into it. If you feel the desire to have an affair and you do not make a decision that you will not get involved in it, then you will be enticed and drawn into an affair.

The evil desire that is not put to death by the power of the Holy Spirit will conceive. It is born in the emotions and it will grow and develop and give birth to sin. When the sin is full grown, it will give birth to death.

It is absolutely necessary that we crucify those desires, that we have self-awareness and we say no to desires and emotions that are not set on God's plans and purposes. We must step out of ourselves and say, "This is not me. It is the sin that lives in me. I hate this and I will not identify with it, even though I feel strong emotions. I hate it and I renounce it. I call it sin and I choose to push it out of my life."

By doing that, you take the sin out of your life so that you won't be snared by those desires. You will be free to fulfill your destiny and to do what God has called you to do. You will be free to walk in the love of God and become a builder of His kingdom, to set your emotions on God's Word and create the emotions God tells you to. You

> The evil desire that is not put to death by the power of the Holy Spirit will conceive.

will have passion for the destiny that God has for you, for His Kingdom, to bring glory to His name and to bear much fruit. We must walk by faith and not be driven by emotions.

How do you bind your emotions to the Word of God? The Bible says that you must walk by faith and not by sight. Your emotions are the link to faith in your life. They link you to faith because faith is in the now. Faith is never in the future. If you are talking about the future, you are not in faith. You might be in hope, but that is not faith. You are not in faith until you can see it now.

*Now faith is the substance of things
hoped for, the evidence of things not seen.*
(Hebrews 11:1 KJV)

God always finishes things before He starts
them. He always sees it done before He can begin
it. When Adam and Eve sinned, God could say,
"I've already won." Jesus was crucified for the
sins of the world before the foundation of the world
(1 Peter 1:20).

Now you can do the same thing. You must
see your victory now, not in the future. You must
see your healing now, not in the future. Your deliverance is now, not in the future. That's how
faith is. It is now.

This is how your emotions serve as a link
to faith. They bring you to that place where
you can see yourself already victorious, already
crossing the finish line. The circumstances no
longer matter.

The thermostat is a big thing in my life. I'm
always cold and my husband Tom is always hot.
When I wake up in the morning, it's sixty degrees in
the room. I don't do well with sixty degrees.

So I decide I need to turn the room into a sau-
na. I go to the thermostat and turn it up to seventy-
six. Even though the thermostat is set at seventy-
six, that doesn't mean that the room is seventy-six.
It takes some time to get there.

But as soon as I set the thermostat, I've already seen the room at seventy-six. I'm looking at the thermostat, not the room. I'm looking at the controls, not the circumstances. And I already feel warmer. I'm planning my activities around a seventy-six-degree room.

When you connect your emotions to the Word of God, it is like turning the thermostat. You set your emotions for seventy-six degrees, that is, you set them on the Word, the environmental control, not on the circumstances around you. Your emotions connect you to faith and the circumstances will follow.

You have to make the transition in life from being led by your feelings to living by faith. Instead of letting your emotions tell you how you feel, you have to tell your feelings how they feel according to the Word of God. You have to direct and train them and develop your emotions to be an asset in the Kingdom of God. You have to direct them so that they are used for good and not for bad in your life.

The key to becoming Spirit-led instead of emotionally-driven is to bind your emotions to the Word. You tell your feelings that this is how they need to be. You are loved because God said you are. So now you draw on the love of God and act like you're loved. You have favor because God has given you favor. So you quit being a victim and you quit whining. You take on the emotions of favor and you act like you have favor. You become generous and you show favor to others. You live by faith instead of by the circumstances. And faith is now.

God told Ezekiel that the people were to stop saying that what God spoke was in the future. It was now.

> *But I the LORD will speak what I will, and it shall be fulfilled without delay. For in your days, you rebellious house, I will fulfill whatever I say, declares the Sovereign LORD.* (Ezekiel 12:25)

God called them a rebellious people because they thought that the fulfillment of God's promises were somewhere far off in the future. If you see it in the future, it will not be fulfilled in your life. So stop saying it is in the future. Faith is now. Speak to your emotions now and bind them to the Word of God now.

You need to understand the power of con-fession. You need to recognize the power of your thoughts and the power of vision. But you also need to see the power of your emotions. They are a vi-tal link to faith. They are an essential part of the puzzle for the fulfillment of God's Word in your life. How do you direct them? You begin to praise God, to thank Him, to bless Him and to proclaim that you already have it. You are already victorious.

The Power of the Subconscious Mind

When I went through nurse's training, there was a period of time when I worked in the mental hospital. We took care of many patients who had nervous breakdowns. What that meant was that their conscious minds collapsed from overwork or exhaustion or other things. When that happened, the subconscious took over. It became impossible for them to know what was real and what was not.

You have two minds. The conscious mind is that part of you that is aware of your surroundings and your circumstances. It knows what is real and what is not real. It makes decisions all day long.

The subconscious mind is very different. It doesn't argue with you. It can't tell what is real and what is not. It can't tell the difference between an actual victory and a good confession. It only hears what you say and it has to respond to that.

If you compared the two minds watching a football game, the conscious mind would be at the game, watching the whole thing in person. The subconscious mind would be somewhere else, listening to the game on the radio. It would have no idea what is happening beyond what it can hear the announcer say. If the announcer gave the wrong name for a player, the subconscious mind would never know. If the announcer says that your team scored a touchdown when they really didn't, the subconscious mind would still cheer. It just wouldn't know any better. It would believe you won the game no matter what actually happened, because it heard shouts of joy and cheering.

The subconscious mind is a place of pure faith. It reacts and it responds to whatever it is told. It takes the information that it is given and it comes into total agreement with the spirit man and conceives the word that it has heard. Your behavior comes out of the subconscious. Pure faith happens.

The problem is that the faith that comes from your subconscious mind is dependent on what your conscious mind tells it. Your subconscious mind is reactive and responds to your emotions. That is the only input that it can get. If your emotions say that you are sad and defeated and that everything is wrong, then your subconscious will take that information and turn it into pure faith. You will find yourself believing that you are sad and defeated and that everything is wrong. And when you believe it, you will have it.

The situation, then, is this. Your behavior comes from your subconscious mind. But your subconscious reacts to your emotions. If your emotions are controlled by your circumstances, then your behavior will be controlled by the circumstances also. Your faith will be tied to your circumstances. You will turn away from what the Word of God says and those emotions will conceive sin and destruction in your life.

Remember, though, that the conscious mind can make decisions. Usually we allow our emotions to tell us how we feel but the conscious mind can override the emotions by dictating to them where they will go. The conscious mind can ignore the circumstances and choose

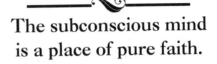

The subconscious mind is a place of pure faith.

to speak what the Word of God says and take on the emotions of joy, praise and rejoicing. It can choose to praise God and to thank Him for His promises.

The subconscious mind will listen to that confession and receive those emotions. It doesn't know any better. When it hears the confession of victory and praise, it assumes that we must have won. The image of a winner is formed in it and that is what it believes. It can't tell when the circumstances are bad. All it knows is the confession that it hears. If that confession is the Word of God with the joy and praise, then pure faith for the things of God is what happens. The subconscious mind takes that confession and comes into agreement with the spirit man over it. Godly behavior is conceived—and the emotions follow along. They really don't have a choice.

When you are cheering, the subconscious can't tell whether you are doing it because you won or just because you are in obedience to the Word of God. It just knows what it hears.

The subconscious mind is a storage place. It is where all of your hopes, your dreams, your fears, past experiences and your beliefs are kept. It runs your whole body. It is the power plant for hormones, your organs, your heartbeat and your breathing. It keeps order. But it is reactive and responsive to what it hears.

That is why the Word tells you to always rejoice and count it all joy in hard times and in trials. When your subconscious hears and feels all that joy and rejoicing, it declares that you have won and you've got the victory. It's already happened and it enters into pure faith and the promises, not the circumstances. You must consciously determine what your subconscious will hear. Is it going to hear the confession of your uncontrolled negative emotions or is it going to hear and feel the confession of joy and rejoicing with God's Word? You are the only one who can decide that.

God wants you to start your day with a conscious decision to have a positive attitude based on the Word. As you confess that attitude, it will direct your thoughts. Your thoughts will create emotions. Your emotions will create the image in your subconscious and your subconscious will give birth to your behavior. If you do not have good behavior, you have to change it by placing your emotions on the things of God.

This will affect everything that you do in life. I can remember the first time that I was asked to read something in front of a group of people. I was in the second grade. A fear gripped me and I just froze. That fear followed me all of my life. Whenever I would read, I was terrified of pronouncing a word wrong and I just couldn't do it.

But God called me to preach His Word, so I had to overcome it. Every time the fear came, I said, "No, I'm a winner. I'm a great reader and I can do it. I'm excellent at pronouncing words." All my subconscious mind knows is what I tell it. If I tell it I can read, then it will produce the behavior and I will read.

Choosing Courage

The Bible is filled with examples of people who directed their emotions and gained victory. There were many times that God told people to sing as they were going into battle. They were to praise and rejoice. It created a response in their subconscious minds and the behavior that resulted was that of a winner.

When Joshua prepared to lead the people into the Promised Land, God told him exactly where he needed to place his emotions. It was not to be fear.

Have I not commanded you? Be strong and courageous. Do not be terrified; do not be discouraged, for the LORD your God will be with you wherever you go. (Joshua 1:9)

God told Joshua that no emotions of fear were to be allowed. There would be no discouragement or dismay. He was going into battle and he was to set his emotions on victory, success and courage. He was to focus on only the promises that God made to get the enemy off of his land.

What Joshua did was very different from what the ten spies did forty years earlier. When Moses sent them in to spy out the land, they did not prepare themselves. They did not confess victory and success. As a result, the behavior that was produced from the subconscious was that of a loser. They saw themselves as small and defeated. They had a slave mentality. Their report was from the emotions of fear and discouragement.

> *But the men who had gone up with him said, "We can't attack those people; they are stronger than we are." And they spread among the Israelites a bad report about the land they had explored. They said, "The land we explored devours those living in it. All the people we saw there are of great size. We saw the Nephilim there (the descendants of Anak come from the Nephilim). We seemed like grasshoppers in our own eyes, and we looked the same to them.*
> (Numbers 13:31-33)

Joshua and Caleb were the only ones who saw it differently. They had set their emotions on the promises of God and when they reported, they sounded very different from the other ten who went with them.

> *Then Caleb silenced the people before Moses and said, "We should go up and take possession of the land, for we can certainly do it."* (Numbers 13:30)

Unfortunately, the ten prevailed and the Israelites wandered in the wilderness for forty years, all because they failed to put their emotions on the Word of God. They walked in fear and failure rather than victory and success.

It is interesting to see the contrast between what the ten spies thought and what the people in the land of Canaan thought. The ten believed that the people saw them as grasshoppers but when Joshua sent two spies into Jericho, they got a very different report from one of the residents.

Rahab was a prostitute who lived in a room in the wall of Jericho. Joshua's spies spoke with her about the state of the city.

> *Before the spies lay down for the night, she went up on the roof and said to them, "I know that the LORD has given this land to you and that a great fear of you has fallen on us, so that*

all who live in this country are melting in fear because of you. We have heard how the LORD dried up the water of the Red Sea for you when you came out of Egypt, and what you did to Sihon and Og, the two kings of the Amorites east of the Jordan, whom you completely destroyed. When we heard of it, our hearts melted and everyone's courage failed because of you, for the LORD your God is God in heaven above and on the earth below. (Joshua 2:8-11)

That does not sound like the confession of a people who saw the Israelites as grasshoppers. The ten spies saw circumstances that were not the truth. They failed to take the promises God had for them because they were driven by the emotions of fear and discouragement. Joshua and Caleb chose to place their emotions on the promises of God and they succeeded. They were ready to fight and overcome and Jericho didn't stand a chance after that.

Your emotions link you to faith and cause faith to happen in you. When you take on the right emotions of joy, rejoicing, praising and even leaping for joy, your subconscious says, "We won," and your behavior reflects that confidence. Your subconscious responds to the emotions and it creates victory in your life.

If you don't set your emotions somewhere, the circumstances in life will set them somewhere for you and that won't be good.

8

Selfish Encounters With God

One day Jesus took Peter, James and John up to a mountaintop to pray. It turned into one of those glorious times of spiritual manifestation that Christians love to experience.

> *There he was transfigured before them. His face shown like the sun, and his clothes became as white as the light. Just then there appeared before them Moses and Elijah, talking with Jesus.* (Matthew 17:2-3)

The three disciples were overwhelmed. It's not every day that you see the glory of God revealed like that and to see Moses and Elijah on top of that must have been amazing. They did what most of us would do.

> *Peter said to Jesus, "Lord, it is good for us to be here. If you wish, I will put up three shelters—one for you, one for Moses and one for Elijah."* (Matthew 17:4)

When we have those wonderful mountaintop experiences, like Peter, we want to hang on to them. There is nothing like being in the presence of God and feeling the power of the Holy Spirit moving. It is exhilarating and exciting.

However, Jesus put it all into perspective. Luke tells us that Peter didn't know what he was saying (Luke 9:33). While Jesus did not say it in those words, He also didn't let Peter build shelters or altars or anything else. In fact He told the three disciples not to even talk to anyone about what they had seen.

> *As they were coming down the mountain, Jesus instructed them, "Don't tell anyone what you have seen, until the Son of Man has been raised from the dead."* (Matthew 17:9)

There was to be no shrine erected to commemorate the event. There was to be no bragging about how spiritual they were because God had shown them this marvelous sight. And above all, Jesus didn't want them to stay there. He led them back down the mountain. There was ministry to do. There was a boy who needed deliverance from a demon waiting at the foot of the mountain.

It wasn't that the mountaintop experience was bad. Jesus was the one who led them there in the first place. However, He demonstrated that it was a selfish thing to stay there, even when the emotions were good. When you are emotionally-driven instead of Spirit-led, even positive emotions can turn into selfishness.

We are learning that we need to use our emotions for what God intended them to do. We are to direct them into what God has commanded. He commanded us to rejoice, to be happy and to be full of joy. We are to bring life wherever we go and to be full of love for God and His people.

> When you are emotionally-driven instead of Spirit-led, even positive emotions can turn into selfishness.

Emotions bring life when they are set on the things of God. When we live in joy, we can impart joy. When we laugh, we can impart laughter. When we live in favor, we can impart favor. When we live in the love of God, we can impart that love. We have a responsibility to set the atmosphere around us with our emotions.

Tom always did that in our home. He didn't allow wrong emotions. He always had a joke. He filled our home with laughter. He always brought fun. He was never a moody man. He set the emotional tone of the entire house in the direction that God desired. And that brought life to the family. He was always concerned about the family and how to give love and value to others. He was never selfish. It was never about him.

Healthy emotions are not just about you feeling good. They are about accomplishing God's purpose in you and through you. They are intended to connect you to faith so that you can do God's will in your life. That doesn't mean you shouldn't enjoy emotions. But it does mean that you shouldn't be selfish with them.

Spiritual encounters with God can be times of encouragement that prepare us to impart life to others. Or they can become perverted into selfish and self-centered emotional highs that do not give value to others. Many Christians become addicted to encounters with God. They so love the emotions of that experience that they become almost like a drug addict. They will do anything to get that experience. They will go anywhere and they will stay in meetings all night if they need to, just to get an emotional high.

Please understand that I am not speaking against personal encounters with God. I have had many mountaintop experiences myself. But there is a purpose for those times. When we are with God, He imparts to us—spiritual gifts and revelations— and we are then to take those things and impart them to others. Freely we have received and we should freely give. If we stay in the encounter without using the impartations for the purposes of God, then we are selfish. We must always keep in mind what God is trying to accomplish through us. Too often, we experience that emotional high that comes with God's presence and we just want to stay there forever—and we try to do so. It becomes perverted because it is selfish. It's all about me.

This principle is true for virtually every area of life. Consider food, for example. God has given us food to eat and we all need that, but we are supposed to eat to live, not live to eat. When we begin to eat just for the emotional high of enjoying food, we become gluttons. The purpose of food becomes perverted through selfishness. Work is good.

> God never intended for us to have a continuous camp meeting.

God made mankind to work. But when someone becomes a workaholic, it turns work into a perverted and selfish experience. God gave us sex to be an important and beautiful part of marriage, but if you become addicted to the emotional high from it, you can turn it into a selfish and perverted thing that causes harm.

God loves to give us personal encounters with Him and He loves to impart special gifts to us. But He doesn't give them to us for selfishness just so we can look for highs all the time. God never intended for us to have a continuous camp meeting. He never expected us to run from one meeting to the next constantly looking for that ecstasy of godly encounters. Such people become so self-absorbed that they enter into a kind of spiritual pride in their lives.

It is always sad to see people who have a certain experience with the Lord and revel in it and then, they go to a restaurant and they are so rude and unkind to the waitress that you are embarrassed about just being with them. The precious spiritual gifts that God gave them have become perverted through selfishness. They have taken something good and made it ugly.

When Tom and I were young in the Lord, we were involved in children's ministry. We were in a church that loved to have services that started at eight o'clock in the morning and kept going until three o'clock in the afternoon. And we had their children during that whole time.

By noon, the kids were climbing the walls. They were tired of being there. They were hungry. They were mad. They were beating each other up. They had heard as many stories about Jesus as they were going to listen to.

But their parents came to pick them up, just glowing because of the wonderful time that they had with Jesus. They spoke of how great the anointing was. Tom would point out that they were selfish. They were getting high at the expense of their children. They were teaching their children that church was a miserable place where they were forced to stay far longer than any child could reasonably be expected to enjoy, night after night for weeks and months at a time, without any home life or family time. They were driving their children away from God. They were abusing their children. It should not be a surprise when such kids grow up and don't want anything to do with church.

It would impart a greater sense of the goodness of God if you took your kids home, fed them, gave them a nap and let them play. Then in your private time or when the kids go to bed, you can continue with your own encounter with God. I'm not saying that you can't have worship time with your children. You should, but don't abuse them with church. Church is good and kids should learn to go but if you keep them there too much and for too long, what they will learn is that God keeps them locked up and separated from their parents. That is a perversion of the truth and it is not the destiny God has for them.

When you live your life in pursuit of those emotional spiritual highs, you become dependent on them. The day that you don't feel the emotions, you think that God is mad at you and you start to worry and chase after the emotions. You become a spiritual yo-yo. When you don't feel the emotion, you think you've done something wrong, so you're up and down and your life becomes based on the feeling, not on the Word of God.

God wants you to bind your emotions to the Word. When you do that, it doesn't matter what you're feeling. You live by the Word, not by the emotions. It doesn't matter if you feel God or not. I know that God loves me because the Word says so. I know that God will never leave me or forsake me, whether I feel His presence or not. If I don't feel those emotions right now, I know that as long as I bind myself to the Word, the emotions will come. But I am not dependent on them. I don't question whether or not God is mad at me. I know that He is not.

We all have days when we don't feel especially spiritual, but we don't live by that. We live by the Word of God. The Word tells us that we are His special treasure and that He has good things for us, no matter what we feel like and no matter what the circumstances are. Binding our emotions to the Word of God brings stability.

God is generous and we are made in His image. So we need to learn to be generous, too. We have encounters with God. There are special times when He imparts gifts to us. In those moments, we need to take those gifts, open them and then go and give them away.

There was a particular time when God visited me and I felt waves and waves of His love coming over me. It was a wonderful experience, an emotional high. I wanted it to go on for the rest of my life. But once He had given it to me, I needed to be a giver of it. I got to enjoy it, but then I needed to be generous with it. I reap what I sow. If I sow it, then God can bring more.

But I had to die to myself. I had to realize that my life is not about emotional highs. It is about passing the love of God on to others. It isn't about me being super special. It's about what I can now give and what I can do to be faithful to the work the Lord has given me.

When I first got saved, I had many wonderful experiences with God. But it didn't make me any better than anyone else. I didn't go from meeting to meeting to try and maintain that emotional high. Rather, I now use what God gave me to impart to others.

Generosity in Paul's Life

Paul had an encounter with God on the road to Damascus. It was a memorable and miraculous experience. Over the next several days, God imparted a calling and a vision to Paul that was exciting and tremendous. Ananias visited him and through Ananias, God told Paul that he was to be a voice to the Gentiles and a spokesman to kings. Paul was blinded and then miraculously restored. It was an awesome encounter with God that involved healing and prophetic words.

Paul could have spent the rest of his life running from meeting to meeting to try and stay in that moment and always experience the presence of God. Instead, his encounters with God led him into his ministry. He couldn't wait to pass on what God had given him. In Romans, he expressed where his heart really was. It was not in chasing after encounters with God.

> *For I long to see you, that I may impart to you some spiritual gift, so that you may be established—that is, that I may be encouraged together with you by the mutual faith both of you and me.* (Romans 1:11-12 NKJV)

Paul understood that when he had that encounter with God, the impartation that he received was not there for him alone. He did not become self-absorbed and allow the experience to become an addiction. He did not pervert what God gave him and chase after it at the expense of everyone around him. Instead, he took what God gave him and looked for opportunities to give it away.

The word "impart" means to give, to share, to distribute. The word implies being generous in what God has given to you. It is to give with a cheerful overflow. It means not only giving but getting excited and cheerful about it. You can't wait to share it.

Paul wanted to establish them. The New International Version says, "to make you strong." When God gave him something, Paul immediately thought about how he could use it to strengthen and establish others. Your focus needs to be the same. God gives something to you so that you can give it away. By giving it away, you open the door for God to give you even more. He does it so that you can establish others. You can establish them in the love of God because God has given you love. When God gives you something, you want to give it away so that you can establish those you encounter, strengthen them and make them steadfast.

_____ ❧ _____

As you impart spiritual gifts to others, you connect to them and now you're a whole team.

_____

Paul goes on to say that he wants to impart something to the believers in Rome so that he may be encouraged with them. That word "encourage" means several things. It means that together we will be strengthened. Together we will be comforted. We will be united together. There is a process of strengthening and uniting that takes place.

So it isn't just a matter of you giving out. It creates a connection. You're not alone in what God's given you but as you impart spiritual gifts to others, you connect to them and now you're a whole team growing together in the love of God.

Paul created a team by imparting to others and then sending them out to do the same thing. Timothy became a believer under the ministry of Paul. Paul was his spiritual father and he had imparted a spiritual gift when he laid hands on Timothy. Timothy became a pastor and Paul wrote to him to tell him not to sit on that gift but to use it for the good of others.

> *Do not neglect your gift, which was given you through a prophetic message when the body of elders laid their hands on you. Be diligent in these matters; give yourself wholly to them, so that everyone may see your progress.*
> (1 Timothy 4:14-15)

Paul reminded Timothy that he is to be diligent. The New King James Version translates it as "meditate on these things." Timothy was to pay attention to the impartation that he received because that was where his progress was. In the next letter, Paul again tells him to "fan into flame the gift of God, which is in you through the laying on of my hands" (2 Timothy 1:6). Just a few verses later, he made it clear that fanning the gift into flame meant giving it away.

> *And the things you have heard me say in the presence of many witnesses entrust to reliable men who will also be qualified to teach others.* (2 Timothy 2:2)

Paul received from God and he passed it on to Timothy. What Timothy received, he was to pass on to others and then teach them to pass it on as well.

As we have encounters with God, we are not to keep it to ourselves and revel in the emotional high of that experience. We are to give it away at the first opportunity. You cannot stay on a mountaintop and ever hope to accomplish the will of God.

It is important to go to meetings and experience God. But when it becomes something that you are driven to and it is abusing others, it is like a drug. You need to get high on God and, just like a drug addict, you will start to abuse your family, your children, your friends and the people around you, just so you can get that high. Instead of living like that, you need to die to yourself and you need to learn how to take the gifts of God and give them away.

Abiding in the Word

John 1:1 tells us that Jesus is the Word of God. We need to be sure that we are binding our emotions to the Word—to Jesus—reading the Word, meditating on it and not just looking for the next high. Jesus said it this way.

> *Abide in Me, and I in you. As the branch cannot bear fruit of itself, unless it abides in the vine, neither can you, unless you abide in Me. I am the vine, you are the branches. He who abides in Me, and I in him, bears much fruit; for without Me you can do nothing.* (John 15:4-5 NKJV)

Jesus says that He is the Word and unless you abide in the Word, you cannot do anything. You can't bear any fruit. And God has called us all to bear fruit for His glory.

In other words, God is saying to you, "All the things that I've called you to do, your destiny and the success that I have for you, will never happen outside of the Word of God." If you are not connected to the Word because you are running from meeting to meeting, looking for a spiritual high, you will never be able to see your destiny happen. If you are not allowing that Word to go through your life and bear fruit for God's glory, then you will never be what God created you to be.

The fruit that God wants to produce in you is the fruit of the Spirit—love, joy, peace, patience, kindness, goodness, faithfulness, gentleness and self-control (Galatians 5:22-23). He wants to produce love in you so that you can share that love with others. That's how we win the world, not by being religious, not be getting caught up in some super high and running from place to place and neglecting our homes and families.

If the only thing the world sees is our addiction to spiritual highs but they don't see the fruit of the Spirit in our lives, they will never want any part of the Kingdom of God. When they see someone shouting praises to God one minute and then in the next breath speaking abusive words to their children, they will not be able to recognize the love of God.

People who learn to give away what God gives them are people who have bound themselves and their emotions to the Word of God. They are stable. They are representing Jesus by sharing Him through their actions. It is the Word of God that makes all the difference. And Jesus is the Word.

> *The Son is the radiance of God's glory and the exact representation of his being, sustaining all things by his powerful word.* (Hebrews 1:3)

God says that He sustains all things by bringing life to them through the power of the Word. If we want to bring life to any situation, we can only do it the way God does — through the power of the Word. The Amplified Bible calls it "upholding and maintaining and guiding and propelling the universe by His mighty word of power."

We want those encounters with God, but not for selfish gain, not for selfish glorification but rather so that we can give them away for the benefit of the Kingdom of God. It is the Word of God that gives us the power to harness our emotions and set them on the things of God. It is only because of the Word that we can overcome.

I write to you, young men,
because you are strong,
and the word of God lives in you,
and you have overcome the evil one.
(1 John 2:14b)

You overcome the wicked one through the power of the Word and you overcome wicked emotions through the power of the Word. You bind yourself to the Word and you bind your emotions to the Word. The Word will always create stability in your life. It will make you healthy in every way, including emotionally, and you will become a blessing to others.

When that happens, you will stop being selfish with your mountaintop experiences and you will give away the gifts that God imparts to you during those encounters with him. You will learn to value what God gives you and selfishness will disappear from your life.

9
Godly Guilt

Guilt is something that we have all felt at one time or another. How we handle it can have a great impact on our lives. There is a worldly kind of guilt that brings destruction and we need to be free of that. But there is also a godly kind of guilt that warns us something is wrong and leads us to repentance.

King Saul gives us a good example of the wrong way to react to guilt. Throughout most of his reign as king of Israel, Saul found himself at war with one or more of the neighboring countries. One of those wars was against the Amalekites. Through the prophet Samuel, God gave him very specific instructions and a promise of great victory.

> *This is what the LORD Almighty says: "I will punish the Amalekites for what they did to Israel when they waylaid them as they came up from Egypt. Now go, attack the Amalekites and totally destroy everything that belongs to them. Do not spare them; put to death men and women, children and infants, cattle and sheep, camels and donkeys."* (1 Samuel 15:2-3)

Saul set out to obey God and the result was a complete victory over this enemy of Israel. The problem was that Saul did not continue to obey God. He did not destroy everything.

> *He took Agag king of the Amalekites alive, and all his people he totally destroyed with the sword. But Saul and the army spared Agag and the best of the sheep and cattle, the fat calves and lambs — everything that was good. These they were unwilling to destroy completely, but everything that was despised and weak they totally destroyed.* (1 Samuel 15:8-9)

Samuel was quick to respond to Saul. He went to meet him early in the morning. Saul was clearly guilty of disobedience but he did what most people do when confronted by their own guilt. He denied that he had done anything wrong.

> *When Samuel reached him, Saul said, "The LORD bless you! I have carried out the LORD's instructions."* (1 Samuel 15:13)

Samuel's sarcastic reply confronted Saul with the fact that he had not done what God said at all.

> *But Samuel said, "What then is this bleating of sheep in my ears? What is this lowing of cattle that I hear?"* (1 Samuel 15:14)

Saul tried to defend himself. He still wouldn't admit that he was wrong. He tried to make it sound like he was doing a spiritual thing, keeping the spoils so that he could give a sacrifice.

> *Saul answered, "The soldiers brought them from the Amalekites; they spared the best of the sheep and cattle to sacrifice to the* LORD *your God, but we totally destroyed the rest."* (1 Samuel 15:15)

Samuel would hear none of it. He didn't even let Saul finish with his explanation.

> *"Stop!" Samuel said to Saul. "Let me tell you what the* LORD *said to me last night."* (1 Samuel 15:16)

Samuel reminded Saul that God had told him specifically to destroy the Amalekites completely and Saul had not done it. He had disobeyed the LORD. Saul again protested that he was innocent because he did what God said.

"But I did obey the LORD," Saul said. "I went on the mission the LORD assigned me. I completely destroyed the Amalekites and brought back Agag their king. The soldiers took sheep and cattle from the plunder, the best of what was devoted to God, in order to sacrifice them to the LORD your God at Gilgal." (1 Samuel 15:20-21)

Samuel threw it right back in Saul's face with one of the most sobering passages in the Bible.

Does the LORD delight in burnt offerings and sacrifices
*   as much as in obeying the voice of the LORD?*
To obey is better than sacrifice,
*   and to heed is better than the fat of rams.*
For rebellion is like the sin of divination,
*   and arrogance like the evil of idolatry.*
Because you have rejected the word of the LORD,
*   he has rejected you as king.*
(1 Samuel 15:22-23)

Only then, when Saul could no longer avoid the results of his disobedience, did he finally admit that he had sinned. But even then, he did the second thing that most people do when confronted by their own guilt. Rather than repent, he tried to blame it on someone else.

> *Then Saul said to Samuel, "I have sinned. I violated the LORD's command and your instructions. I was afraid of the people and so I gave in to them.* (1 Samuel 15:24)

He tried to convince Samuel to come back with him to worship God but Samuel refused. There was no repentance in Saul. First there was denial, then blame-shifting and self-justification, but he never did repent.

The Warning Sign

If you are driving along in your car and you see a flashing light on a sign that says not to go in a certain direction, you know that it is a warning. If you don't heed that warning, you might end up driving over a cliff or into a river. The sign is a warning to you.

Suppose you are driving along and a red light comes on in your dashboard telling you that you need oil. You stop the car and pull over, open the hood and cut the wire to the light and then get back in the car and keep driving, thinking everything is okay because the red light is off. That would be how denial works in your life. The red light, guilt from God, is on, saying that something is wrong. The denial is like cutting the wire. The problem is still there and you are heading for destruction. But denial won't let you know.

Godly guilt is just such a warning. It comes specifically so that you can recognize the road you are on is going the wrong way and you can repent.

This is a significant part of the work that the Holy Spirit does.

> *When he comes, he will convict the world of guilt in regard to sin and righteousness and judgment.* (John 16:8)

The conviction of the Holy Spirit never condemns us. It warns us. It is an exciting thing in our lives. When we are convicted of guilt in regard to our sin, it means that we can repent and clean out one more thing that is holding us back from God's best for us.

I love it when the Holy Spirit points out to me something that is wrong in my life, when He uses that guilt to reveal things to me. I get excited because of the reward. I know that I will be better after I have repented and gotten that sin out of my life.

There are several benefits to repentance. It means that I'm not going to hurt the heart of God. It is just like with your children. When they do something that is bringing destruction in their lives, it hurts your heart. Repentance means that you are turning away from hurting the heart of God.

Repentance also means that you are getting rid of something in your life that is dangerous and destructive. Repentance means that you are going to the next level. You are going to go in a different direction.

There are three things that you can do when godly guilt comes into your life. You can do what Saul did, meaning that you deny you did anything wrong. Or you can blame it all on someone else. Yes, you did it, but you couldn't help it.

> Repentance also means that you are getting rid of something in your life that is dangerous and destructive.

Either one of these responses to guilt will bring torment into your life, just like it did for Saul. He spent the last part of his life in constant misery from a tormenting spirit. He lived in a paranoid fear that others would take his place. He was absolutely miserable. He wouldn't admit his responsibility and repent.

The third thing that you can do is to repent. You can admit that you are wrong and then give it over to God and change. Ninety-five percent of the people in mental hospitals are suffering from guilt. They just won't bring themselves to repentance.

King David is an interesting contrast to Saul. David did some terrible things in his life. For example, he got another man's wife pregnant and then had her husband killed. Yet he is still described as a man after God's own heart.

How could an adulterous murderer be a man after God's own heart? It was because David had a repentant heart. He did not try to justify his sin or cover it up or deny that it was there. Instead, he admitted it and repented. He understood that forgiveness came when he repented and he wrote these words to express how important it was to him.

> *Then I acknowledged my sin to you*
> *and did not cover up my iniquity.*
> *I said, "I will confess*
> *my transgressions to the LORD" —*
> *and you forgave*
> *the guilt of my sin.*
>
> (Psalm 32:5)

David was forgiven and the guilt of his sin was short-lived. He pushed it away and he was free from it.

God wants us to become responsible. He wants us to acknowledge our problems in life that are caused by the choices we have made. He wants us to recognize the direction we are going. He wants us to realize that we are creating our own experience. He wants us to be accountable. It is only then that we can repent and enter into that place where we can fulfill our destiny.

You can tell when there are situations in your life that don't line up with the Word of God. That godly guilt is there, warning you and pointing out the problem. The Word becomes the very thing that exposes what needs to be changed. This is what John said Jesus came into the world to do.

> *The true light that gives light to every man*
> *was coming into the world.* (John 1:9)

The true light that gives light to every man creates life by shining on the problem areas to expose what is holding us back. It brings into the open everything that is destructive so that we can repent and change.

Godly guilt is not a time for sorrow. It is cause for rejoicing. The sorrow of confronting your guilt is good because it leads you to repentance and repentance leads to life. Paul found reason to be happy in such a situation. On one occasion, he had to write a very strong letter of correction to the church in Corinth because of some things that they allowed in their midst. Afterwards, they repented and changed.

*Even if I caused you sorrow by my letter,
I do not regret it. Though I did regret it—I
see that my letter hurt you, but only for a little
while—yet now I am happy, not because you
were made sorry, but because your sorrow led
you to repentance.* (2 Corinthians 7:8-9)

Paul said that there is no sorrow in the repentance that comes from godly guilt. It is sorrow that is short-lived because it opens the door for the Holy Spirit to clean house and bring life in to replace the sin.

Paul did not regret their sorrow when it led to repentance. How could he say that? He could say it because he was familiar with repentance. If anyone ever had a reason to have sorrow and regret over what he had done, it would be Paul. He had killed some Christians and put others in jail. He had resisted the gospel and persecuted the children of God. By his own admission, he had sought to destroy the church of God (Galatians 1:13).

Yet in spite of all that he had done, Paul declared, "I am innocent of the blood of all men" (Acts 20:26). He could do that because he understood forgiveness. He knew that when he repented and asked God to forgive him, the sin was completely removed. He knew what God said in Psalm 103.

As far as the east is from the west,
  so far has he removed our transgressions
  from us.

(Psalm 103:12)

God says, "I forgive you and I forget the sin." Your sins are blotted out as though you never did them. They are forgiven because you repented. Paul walked in that forgiveness and was completely cleansed of the sin as soon as he confessed it and repented.

If we confess our sins, he is faithful and just and will forgive us our sins and purify us from all unrighteousness. (1 John 1:9)

That means that when you repent, you will be free from the destructive behavior pattern that dominated your life before. You will be free of the thoughts and the attitudes that were so destructive.

I remember when I was a new Christian. I did not want God to tell me that I was doing something wrong. When He did, it was a huge event in my life. I felt that I had to do penance and whip myself for at least two or three days and cry and wail before God so that I could earn forgiveness. All that time, I couldn't do anything useful because I was in a pit of depression. I felt that I was no good.

But the Holy Sprit was gracious. He said to me, "It's a free gift, Maureen. It's by faith, not be feeling. You don't have to punish yourself. Just repent and move on." When we don't understand God's divine forgiveness, we take the guilt and we milk it to the end and we get condemned and then we get depressed and feel so worthless that it takes weeks for us to get back to where God can use us for anything. That is not the way God wants it. He forgives and He forgets and it is by faith that we receive it.

Overwhelming Guilt

Guilt is to be short-lived in our lives. It brings good to us when we acknowledge the sin and then repent. If we don't repent, it creates destruction. Without repentance, the sin stays and so does the guilt. It creates the feeling in us that we have to do some kind of penance or we just go into denial and try to act like nothing is wrong. The guilt becomes overwhelming. That is what happened to Saul. David wrote about it in Psalms.

> *My guilt has overwhelmed me*
> *like a burden too heavy to bear.*
> (Psalm 38:4)

Judas is an example in the New Testament of a man tormented by guilt, much as Saul was.

> *When Judas, who had betrayed him, saw that Jesus was condemned, he was seized with remorse and returned the thirty silver coins to the chief priests and the elders. "I have sinned," he said, "for I have betrayed innocent blood."*
>
> *"What is that to us?" they replied "That's your responsibility."*
>
> *So Judas threw the money into the temple and left. Then he went away and hanged himself.* (Matthew 27:3-5)

Judas was able to admit that he had sinned, but he did not move into the forgiveness of God that would make that guilt short-lived in his life. Compare that to Peter, who denied Jesus three times. He experienced great remorse from his guilt and the Bible tells us that he wept bitterly (Luke 22:62). Rather than be overwhelmed by it, however, Peter's guilt drove him to repentance and caused him to deal with his own failing. The growth that he experienced was demonstrated on the day of Pentecost when he stood up in the Temple and preached to thousands of people right under the noses of the same people who had condemned Jesus. Judas was overwhelmed. Peter grew into great courage and boldness. The difference was in how they responded to the guilt.

Cain was a man who chose denial instead of repentance. He and his brother Abel both gave offerings to God but Abel's offering was from the fat portion, the best that he had, and Cain's offering was not. God had regard for Abel's offering but not for Cain's. Cain got angry with God. The guilt was there and anger resulted. The Bible says that "his face was downcast" (Genesis 4:5). He was depressed, sad and he felt terrible.

God spoke to Cain and asked him why he was angry. He said, "If you do what is right, will you not be accepted?" (Genesis 4:7). In other words, God made it clear that the reason Cain felt the way he did was because there was something wrong in him. If he repented and admitted that he did not do it the right way, then God would accept him. He would be forgiven. But there was a danger if he did not repent.

> But if you do not do what is right, sin is crouching at your door; it desires to have you, but you must master it. (Genesis 4:7)

Sin doesn't want you to repent because it wants to have you . It wants to control you. But you need to master it. You need to deal with the thoughts and emotions and desires that lead you to sin. You have the power to bring those things under control. If you do not master them, they will master you.

Too often we don't want to admit that we've done anything wrong because we are afraid that God won't accept us. But God already knows you did it wrong and He has already accepted you. He is just waiting for you to admit that you're wrong and repent. When you do, you will be free from the guilt. What keeps us from repentance is pride in our lives that keeps us in denial.

Adam chose to blame others instead of repent. He sinned and God came to the garden and called out to him, "Where are you?" Right away Adam started to make excuses.

> *He answered, "I heard you in the garden, and I was afraid because I was naked; so I hid."* (Genesis 3:10)

He hid because he knew he had done something wrong and he was afraid he was going to get caught. But he was caught. He still didn't say, "Yes, I did it," and repent, however. He started blaming everyone else. It was "the woman you put here with me" (Genesis 3:12). It was Eve's fault. It was God's fault because He was the one who made Eve in the first place.

Unfortunately, people act like Adam all the time. Even when they get to the point that they can admit they did something wrong, they still won't take responsibility for it. They blame their parents or their spouse or their environment or their job or they blame God. For example, they want to make it God's fault that they are sick rather than learning to eat healthy instead of indulging in junk food and starting to exercise instead of sitting around all the time.

God wants you to become accountable for your life and for your decisions. It is time that you grow up. Your mind will always come up with an excuse and it always makes you sound innocent but you must say no to your mind and ask the Holy Spirit to show you what you need to change or what you did wrong. Step into self-awareness. You are an adult now and you can make choices. When you blame others, the sin never goes away and the enemy has opportunity to accuse you. When he does that, you become tormented by the guilt, rather than letting the guilt bring you to repentance.

I understand that bad things may have happened to you earlier in your life. You may have been abused. You may have gone through things that you had no control over. But you do have control over your thoughts and attitudes now and if you do not harness them and bind them to the Word of God, they will bring you destruction. If you do not repent of sin in your life, it will continue to torment you.

I love to repent. I love it when the Holy Spirit puts the guilt of conviction in my life so that I can repent.

Guilt does not have to overwhelm you. Through repentance, it becomes very short-lived in your life and you are set free to move to the next level. You are loosed from those things that are holding you back from your destiny.

10
Anger

I believe that Jesus was Spirit-led and that His emotions were under the control of the Holy Spirit. He filled His environment with love, joy, laughter, excitement, life, fun, peace, kindness and mercy. There was a lot of emotional blessing coming from Jesus.

As He is usually portrayed in movies or television programs, however, Jesus is pictured as quiet, reserved and always in perfect control, with an almost inhuman lack of emotion. Most of the world has this image of Him. He speaks in a slow, measured, monotone voice. He never smiles. He never raises His voice. Everything He says is a profound spiritual revelation. It is hard for most people to imagine Jesus just talking.

There is one significant incident that paints a very different picture of Jesus than most people normally think of. It happened a week before the crucifixion. He came into Jerusalem with the crowds shouting, "Hosanna" and laying palm branches before him. He was more popular than at any time in His public ministry.

Once inside the city, Jesus went into the outer courtyard of the Temple. There He found the money changers. It wasn't so much that they were doing business in the Temple. It was the kind of business that bothered Him. There was a tremendous amount of fraud, over-pricing and corruption attached to the business. They really were a "den of robbers."

Jesus did not react in a passive, quiet way. In fact, He exploded. He made a whip and started swinging. He turned over tables and scattered coins all over the place.

> *Jesus entered the temple area and drove out all who were buying and selling there. He overturned the tables of the money changers and the benches of those selling doves. "It is written," he said to them, "'My house will be called a house of prayer,' but you are making it a 'den of robbers.'"* (Matthew 21:12-13)

Jesus felt anger that day. It was an emotion that resulted from his zeal for His Father's house, for the Temple. In His case, it was valid anger.

We all feel anger. Sometimes it is valid. More often it is not. That does not mean that we do not feel it, however. It is very important that we handle anger properly, whether it is valid or not.

> *In your anger do not sin.* (Ephesians 4:26)

The sin is not in feeling anger. It is in mismanaging it. When you are driven by anger rather than managing it, the result is great destruction.

Anger, like guilt, is another warning sign that something is wrong. It can point to something wrong in you. It can also point to something that is wrong in someone else. The first step in managing anger is to determine what it is that makes you angry and why.

The second step is to bring it under control. Most of us mismanage our anger and it becomes destructive in our lives. But it doesn't have to be that way. The Bible tells us ways to deal with it. Proverbs gives this advice:

> *A gentle answer turns away wrath,*
> *but a harsh word stirs up anger.*
> (Proverbs 15:1)

One translation says a "soft voice" turns away wrath. You need to recognize that the tone of your voice creates an atmosphere that will either encourage anger or discourage it. Husbands, you should not be harsh with your wives. Your words might be technically correct, but the tone in your voice might stir an angry response. It is especially important in a situation where you have to give someone correction or a rebuke, as might happen at work. Your boss might be very angry about something and the work environment is charged with anger. A soft answer will diffuse that atmosphere. Always approach the situation with a soft voice and you will minimize the potential for anger to bring destruction. A harsh word will bring exactly the opposite.

> *An angry man stirs up dissension,*
> *and a hot-tempered one commits many*
> *sins.*
>
> (Proverbs 29:22)

If you give yourself to anger, you will become the cause of dissension and discord. You will cause division. Anger that is allowed to have its full manifestation will bring destruction. It will result in verbal, physical and emotional abuse. Anger must be diffused and handled in a right way. Mismanaged anger does not bring about the righteous life that God desires. Rather, it brings destruction and it breaks relationships.

The Bible says, however that it is possible to be angry and not sin. If Jesus did it, then it must be possible. The secret is learning to manage the anger in a godly, biblical way.

Getting Control

The first thing we should examine is what causes anger. Then we will have a better understanding of what to do in order to harness it.

Anger can be the reaction to a wrong response. You did something really nice for someone and they didn't appreciate it or perhaps you didn't receive what you expected from a relationship. It is possible to be angry with God when you expect something and it doesn't happen.

Rather than just suppress such anger, we need to ask ourselves why we are feeling it. The answer to that question will help determine how to handle the anger. It might just expose something that you need to deal with.

Many years ago, I was diagnosed with rheumatoid arthritis and it developed quickly into a very serious ailment. God miraculously healed me within two months, but there was an anger toward God that I had to deal with. I kept feeling that God should have protected me. I should not have had to go through that suffering. My trust was shaky.

I had to face the fact that it was not God's fault. I got sick because of the way I abused my body. I wasn't eating right. I wasn't sleeping right. I stayed up most of the night praying for the church, night after night. I lived on coffee, cake and cookies. I wasn't eating anything nutritious or even taking vitamins. So, at forty-five, my body collapsed.

It was not God's fault. It was mine. But I had to deal with the anger that I felt toward God. Without that anger, I would not have thought about it enough to deal with my own problem of how I took care of myself. The anger helped expose something that I needed to take care of.

There can be many reasons that you might get angry with God. Perhaps you lost a loved one or you expected a promotion and didn't get it. You might want something now and it hasn't happened yet. We've all had disappointments and we've all expected things that didn't come. There are four other things that create anger:

1. When people are irresponsible by their actions.
2. Their behavior is unfair; they are not carrying their load.
3. People are self-serving.
4. People are disrespectful; they cut us off or change the subject while we are talking.

You need to stop and face your anger. Don't give full vent to it, however. First of all, wait until you calm down. A wise man holds back his anger.

> *Mockers stir up a city,*
>   *but wise men turn away anger.*
> *If a wise man goes to court with a fool,*
>   *the fool rages and scoffs, and there is no*
>   *peace.*
>
> (Proverbs 29:8-9)

It is a fool who rages and the result is that there is no peace. We all have felt anger, but when that anger is released and it gets out of control, when it is mismanaged, then we have stepped over the edge. We must first bring it under control. We must cool down before we act in the flesh and bring destruction.

You need to have a strategy. Plan what you are going to do ahead of time. First of all, get yourself out of that situation. You need to excuse yourself. Go for a walk. Pray in the Holy Spirit. Go for a bike ride. Work in the yard. Work off the adrenaline that is demanding a reaction of rage. Direct it somewhere else. That emotion of rage always wants you to do something extreme and rash. Take it somewhere that it won't hurt anyone or anything.

> We must cool down before we act in the flesh and bring destruction.

Once you've worked off the adrenaline, you can calm down, clear your head and think clearly. You can see that it is not a major event. It is only a minor thing. Then you can find a way to handle the situation.

Types of Anger

There are different kinds of anger. Explosive anger is focused outwardly. When people are explosive with their anger, they become physical with it.

When they're in that moment of anger, they don't take control and harness it and it manifests itself physically. They are ready to fight. They strike out. They enter into verbal abuse. They explode and just tell it like it is.

People with explosive anger usually feel justified because they feel so good after they have exploded. They get it off their chest and it gives them a rush, a high. Of course they leave bodies all around them from the people they have exploded all over. They hurt all kinds of people, but they feel wonderful themselves. They create great destruction and they ruin relationships in the process of giving vent to their anger. They control people through fear. People tip toe around them.

Implosive anger is just as bad. It is emotional abuse. People who have this type of anger do not explode but rather, become a ticking bomb. They withdraw and the anger is turned inward. They would like to say things but it never comes out. Instead they live the outburst in their minds and it builds resentment and bitterness. It creates hatred and it brings rebellion and depression. When we bury anger, it is buried alive.

Such people allow the anger to build up inside until one day they fall into deep depression. In extreme cases, it can manifest itself in murder or suicide. Teenagers have the highest rate of suicide of any age group. The reason is that parents don't teach them how to manage their anger. They just teach them to suppress it and when they try to do that, it leads to depression, which can lead to suicide.

Suppressed anger, even if it does not reach the extreme of suicide, will still cause you to die on the inside. You won't feel the life of God and you will start to experience depression. You will just want to end it all. People who suppress their anger withdraw and become disconnected from God and from other people. They get offended easily. They have conversations going on in their minds all the time that they can't shut off. They may be smiling, but they have totally disconnected and they will slam doors or pout and give you the silent treatment. This type of anger will open the door to addictions because, in the addictions, it is the only time they feel alive.

Both of these types of anger—explosive and implosive—are destructive. If you do not deal with them, they will hurt you and they will hurt people around you. Proverbs advises us to stay away from those who cannot control their anger.

> *Do not make friends with a hot-tempered man,*
> *do not associate with one easily angered.*
> (Proverbs 22:24)

Being around a hot-tempered person can get you into trouble as well. I had a friend in high school whose brother was violent and hot-tempered. He got in the car one time and drove away with his brother. The brother decided to rob a store. The clerk refused to get money from the safe, so my friend's brother killed him, got back in the car and drove away. My friend got thirty years in prison just because he was in the car at the time.

You never know what someone will do when they don't control their anger. You might get in the car with them and they get angry at some other driver. If they lose control and gun the car to 120 miles per hour and drive over a cliff, it won't matter that you had control of your temper. You will be affected by theirs. Uncontrolled anger produces problems.

> *For as churning the milk produces butter,*
> *and as twisting the nose produces blood,*
> *so stirring up anger produces strife.*
> (Proverbs 30:33)

One of the consequences of anger is that it will create a distance in relationships that will not allow closeness. Whether it is explosive anger that drives people away or implosive anger that causes them to distance themselves, uncontrolled anger will destroy intimacy. It's like they have a spray can of mace. Any time that you get to close to them, they spray you with it to drive you away. They can't handle any close relationship because anger is in them and it is ruling their lives.

We talked earlier about King Saul. His anger ruined every relationship in his life. David delivered Saul from a big problem when he confronted Goliath. He became one of Saul's most loyal followers. But all that Saul heard was the people singing that Saul had killed his thousands, but David had killed his ten thousands. Saul became jealous and angry and tried to kill David several times. He threw spears at him. He tried to ambush him at his home. He spent

> You need to acknowledge that you do have anger.

three years of his life devoted to nothing but trying to track David down with an entire army. Eventually he ended up killed by an enemy in battle. Even the relationship with his own son was destroyed. Saul became angry at Jonathan and tried to kill him.

The jails are filled with people who never learned to control their anger. It is absolutely essential that we learn to control our anger and manage it. There are some basic steps that you can take to do that.

First, you have to admit the truth. You need to acknowledge that you do have anger and that you've mismanaged it. What you don't acknowledge, you can't get free of.

Secondly, you need to have a strategy so that you can break the pattern of anger in your life. Plan ahead of time what you will do when you feel anger rising in you. Take time out. Go for a walk. Work out in the gym. Do whatever you have to in order to work the adrenaline off.

Then, after you have cooled off, ask yourself this very important question. What caused the anger? Was it valid or invalid? Was it distorted anger? Did you perceive injustice when there really was none? Did you think someone wronged you when they really didn't? Ask God to reveal to you just what caused the anger.

God may answer that you were just crabby that day. Maybe you got up on the wrong side of the bed. Maybe you're under stress or you're self-absorbed. It may be that the anger has revealed some long-standing character trait that you need to deal with.

If you don't ask this question and deal with invalid anger, you will be doomed to repeat the incident. If you become angry when you are in a bad mood, then you might calm down, but the next time you are in a bad mood, you will get angry again and cause more destruction to your relationships. You have to bow before God, repent and let Him get that thing out of your life. You have to determine that you are not going to behave that way anymore. To be free of the problem, you have to admit that it is there and then repent of it. If there is some generational thing in your life or some habit pattern that you've grown up with, you must take it to God and get rid of it. Renounce it and ask God to cut you free from it and from those ties and attachments of your forefathers.

Being Spirit-led is mostly a matter of learning to die to yourself. The more you die to self, the more you let go of selfishness and self-centeredness and the more you realize that your anger is not valid.

Valid Anger

What happens if the anger is valid? We saw that Jesus was angry and it was not sin. What if you were to ask God to show you the source of your anger and He showed you that you were mistreated and you did need to be angry?

The truth is that we teach people how to treat us. When people behaved in an inappropriate way to Jesus, He confronted them. He did not back down from calling people hypocrites when they were. Even those closest to Him, such as Peter, were not spared if they were out of line. Peter argued with Jesus about going to the cross and Jesus got right in his face and said, "Get behind me, Satan." Jesus made people accountable. It may be that we need to do the same. But there is a right way and a wrong way to do that.

If you recognize that your anger is valid and that you should confront someone, you need to think it through. You must set up a time when you can go to that person and approach them in a validating way.

Tell them that you value the relationship that you have with them. This is important, since invalid anger always destroys relationships. You want to make sure that your valid anger is handled right. It should always build relationships. Admit that you might be missing something or that your perception might be wrong and ask them to help you understand. Approach the discussion with a humble heart, not with an attitude of revenge. You are not trying to get even. Rather you are trying to correct the problem so that it will not do further damage.

You are going to say good things about the person. You are going to spend some time talking about the traits in them that mean a lot to you and you are going to build them up. Never use "you" statements. Any time that you begin to accuse with words like "You did this" or "You said that," you bring condemnation and that will just make them defensive, which will not accomplish what you need to accomplish. Use "I" statements. Tell them, "This is how I perceive the situation. Please help me understand it." You then explain to them how you felt when they acted in the way that they did.

It might go something like this. "I know you're a great person, but I felt rejection when you did this. It made me feel worthless." Then explain what happened.

When you are done talking, listen while they explain their side to you. Take notes. Then practice reflective questioning. Paraphrase what they say back to them so that if you are misunderstanding them, they have a chance to explain themselves. "What I heard you say was . . ." Repeat it in your own words.

Usually people will see that they have really hurt you and they will be sorry. They will ask you to forgive them and admit that they should not have done the thing that they did. Most people do not intentionally attack others.

> You are not trying to get even. Rather you are trying to correct the problem.

Occasionally, however, the person might answer that they don't agree with you. You then have to recognize that everyone is entitled to his or her opinion and you will have to agree to disagree. But, because you have addressed the situation in a biblical way, acting in love, not in uncontrolled anger, you have avoided a great deal of destruction in your life. It is what the Bible tells us to do.

> *Therefore, if you are offering your gift at the altar and there remember that your brother has something against you, leave your gift there in front of the altar. First go and be reconciled to your brother; then come and offer your gift.* (Matthew 5:23-24)

The relationship is the most important thing. Anything in your life that is destroying relationships is not a good thing. Paul put it very simply when he wrote to the church in Rome.

> *If it is possible, as far as it depends on you, live at peace with everyone.* (Romans 12:18)

That command will be impossible to follow if you do not learn to manage your anger.

11
Enmeshment

As Jesus became well known, He began to draw large crowds everywhere He went. There came a point when it bothered His family. They decided that they needed to get Him under control. On one occasion, He drew such a large crowd that He and the disciples didn't even have time to eat. To the family, He clearly needed someone to get Him to act normal.

> *Then Jesus entered a house, and again a crowd gathered, so that he and his disciples were not even able to eat. When his family heard about this, they went to take charge of him, for they said, "He is out of his mind."* (Mark 3:20-21)

They thought Jesus was crazy. He was doing and saying things that created a scene and embarrassed them. Even the teachers of the law were saying that He was demon possessed. Besides that, He was doing things without the family even being involved. He chose the twelve disciples and not one of them was a brother of His. As His family, they put up with it for a while, but enough was enough. They decided that He needed help to draw Him back into the family.

But Jesus was not crazy. He was about the business of fulfilling His destiny. He was doing exactly what He came to earth to do. He made it clear that He would choose to follow His destiny no matter what. If His family was embarrassed by that, then He would have to choose His destiny over them.

> *Then Jesus' mother and brothers arrived. Standing outside, they sent someone in to call him. A crowd was sitting around him, and they told him, "Your mother and brothers are outside looking for you."*
>
> *"Who are my mother and my brothers?" he asked.*
>
> *Then he looked at those seated in a circle around him and said, "Here are my mother and my brothers! Whoever does God's will is my brother and sister and mother."* (Mark 3:31-35)

It was not that Jesus rejected them as His family. He still did the things that were appropriate for a son and a brother to do. Even on the cross, He still saw to it that there was someone to watch after His mother.

However, He also refused to let His family take Him out of His ministry. He absolutely refused to be drawn into a kind of relationship with the family in which they determined His fate and His future. He let God do that.

He spent quality time with them, even though they taunted Him. In John, we see them together and His brothers mocking Him.

> *But when the Jewish Feast of Tabernacles was near, Jesus' brothers said to him, "You ought to leave here and go to Judea, so that your disciples may see the miracles you do. No one who wants to become a public figure acts in secret. Since you are doing these things, show yourself to the world." For even his own brothers did not believe in him.* (John 7:2-5)

Jesus did not follow the direction that His family seemed to want Him to go, even though they manipulated and mocked Him and tried to use guilt to persuade Him.

What Jesus encountered was a condition known as "enmeshment." Everything that we have talked about so far has dealt with the emotions of the individual. But there are many people who never really experience their own emotions. They are so completely wrapped up in the emotions of their family that they have completely lost their own identity. They have become enmeshed.

Self-Identity and Family Roles

The textbook definition of enmeshment is "a pattern of family relationships in which the members of the family become psychologically and emotionally fused together to such an extent that there is no room for individual growth or development." The individual disappears and the family becomes dominant. The individual members lose all sense of self-identity. They are emotionally entangled with the family. They don't know who they are outside of the family.

If someone in the family is depressed, everybody in the family is depressed. If someone is mad at somebody in the family, everyone in the family is mad at them. When you are enmeshed in a family, you are what the family says you are. The family controls you and you end up on an emotional roller coaster because enmeshed families are emotionally driven, not Spirit-led.

God had a specific identity for you when you were created. Before you were even born He had a book written on you. He gave you His divine nature. He called you to be in Christ and to be complete in Christ. You are His workmanship. He has an identity for you that is unique, unlike any other person who has ever lived or ever will live. You are one of a kind.

An enmeshed family, however, tries to give you an identity that is not centered in Christ. It is a role that you are expected to play and if you try to step out of that role, the family will bring tremendous pressure on you to get back in your place.

Every member of an enmeshed family has a label. There is the lost child of the family, the child who doesn't feel like there's a place for him or her in the family. That person is lost within the family.

There is the black sheep. That is the one who is always going off and doing what he or she is not supposed to do. Black sheep cause the family to be in an uproar and cause devastation to come to the family. They keep the family constantly emotionally upset.

> God had a specific identity for you when you were created.

There is the scapegoat of the family. That's the one that gets the blame for everything that goes wrong. A brother might be taking drugs but the scapegoat is blamed for driving the brother to it or somehow not protecting him.

There is the hero of the family. That is the one who is marked for success. He or she gets straight A's in school. That member is the one that the family puts all of their value into. That is the one that they hold out as the hero who will become an Olympic star or the President or a CEO. They are the best. That person has to perform.

Everyone has a role, but none of them can be who God created them to be. They have to be what the family assigns to them. All the energy of the enmeshed family goes into the family. They over perform for the family and there is no energy left for anything else. They are not supposed to be individuals.

We can use the example of what happens in the natural realm when sexual relationships are not healthy. In marriage, sex is supposed to be an important part of the relationship. When sex starts to happen outside of the relationship between husband and wife and it includes other family members, it is called incest. What was right and good between husband and wife becomes a terrible sin. It is dysfunctional and it is a perversion and it causes great harm because it attacks the identity and the purpose of the family members. God never planned for it to be that way.

When we were born again, we became part of the body of Christ. Every one of us has a place in God, a destiny that is unique to the individual. We are to be enmeshed in Christ, not in the plans and purposes of an earthly family. In Him we find our destiny and the more we entangle ourselves with Him, the more we will fulfill His purpose.

We are to be entangled with Christ. He covers us and gives us all that we need. He pours His love into us and His favor and His joy and His goodness and peace. All of our emotional needs are met in Him. We are a fortified city in Christ and we draw from Him.

In an enmeshed family, the members draw those emotional needs from the wrong place. It becomes an emotional incest because it is an unhealthy tie that destroys the destiny and the uniqueness of the individuals.

Until he is free of enmeshment, the member of the family is always looking to the family for emotional fulfillment. Enmeshed families are driven by guilt. They use guilt to control one another and the guilt creates fear. They are afraid that if they don't do what the family says, then they will be rejected or abandoned. They will become the family outcaste. They are easily manipulated by fear and guilt.

The constant cry of the heart from enmeshed family members is, "Who am I?" Such a person is never able to find the uniqueness that God created for him or her because the family is always pulling them back in. Whenever they try to step away, the family uses fear and guilt to keep them from leaving.

It is like putting your car on cruise control. You can set it for seventy miles per hour. If you speed up to eighty, as soon as you let up on the accelerator, the cruse control brings the car back to seventy. You can never get very far away. You want to be healthy. You want to be what God created you to be. You want to fulfill your destiny. But as soon as you take off, the family pulls you back.

Freedom From Enmeshment

It is only by the power of the Holy Spirit that you can get free of enmeshment. When you step into Christ, He will set you free and you can break those ties.

However, when you determine that you will no longer be the lost child or the scapegoat and you defy the family and the identity that they placed on you, they will escalate. To them, it feels just like a death has occurred. Just as it happened to Jesus, they will think you have lost your mind. They will enter into grief as though you actually died. There will be mourning and sadness. It is all a part of the guilt with which they try to draw you back to your assigned place.

I have a close friend who came from an en-meshed family. She was the scapegoat. As a very small child she said no to the scapegoat and became the lost child instead. But she was still affected by the emotions of being enmeshed in that family. And they tried to mold her into a role.

There was a time as an adult that my friend had to deal with her desire to perform for the family. One day, as she was standing in front of the bath-room mirror, God gave her a vision of what was happening to her. It was like there was a little string hanging down and she was hanging from that string. There was a pair of scissors and she was afraid to do wrong because she believed that the family would cut the string. But God said to her, "Cut it yourself. Just cut the string and be free."

She did step out of that enmeshment and her family did escalate and go through grief and mourning. They acted as though she had died and lamented that she wasn't in the family anymore. But she was in Christ and she wasn't going back. She was finished with the scapegoat and she was finished with the lost child and she was finished with the rejection. God gave her a whole new identity and it didn't fit with the role that the family wanted her to fill.

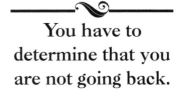
You have to determine that you are not going back.

My friend realized just how much this was true when her brother one day said to her, "I miss my sister. Where are you?"

She told him that she was done with the enmeshment and that her identity was now in Christ. He told her that what really bothered him about the whole thing was that she was never marked for success. Her role was to be the scapegoat.

She had been marked by the family and she was not supposed to be the one who succeeded. And it bothered the family when she did have great success.

You have to determine that you are not going back. You have stepped into Christ and now you are clothed in Him. You are complete in Him. You are fortified in Him and you have that protection over you. As it says in Galatians 2:20, you have been crucified with Christ and it is no longer you who lives but Christ who lives in you.

If you do not leave the enmeshment of the family, you are putting the family before God and before His calling in your life. You have made the family an idol. And Jesus very plainly described how He felt about that.

> *Anyone who loves his father or mother more than me is not worthy of me; anyone who loves his son or daughter more than me is not worthy of me.* (Matthew 10:37)

He also made it clear that there is a reward for those who break free of enmeshment.

> *"I tell you the truth," Jesus replied, "no one who has left home or brothers or sisters or mother or father or children or fields for me and the gospel will fail to receive a hundred times as much in this present age . . . and in the age to come."* (Mark 10:29-30)

It does not mean that you never speak to your family again. You are still to love them. When you are free, you will be able to really love them. You are able to love them with unconditional love. Galatians cautions us to be careful to continue in love.

*You, my brothers, were called to be free.
But do not use your freedom to indulge the sin-
ful nature; rather, serve one another in love.*
(Galatians 5:13)

We do not reject our blood family or abandon them, but we stop looking to them for our identity. It is as though our emotions are like live electrical wires. When they had no insulation, everything they touched caused hurts and wounds. In an enmeshed family, those emotions were always exposed. But once we find our true identity in Christ, He insulates those emotions. He covers them so that nothing the family says or does has the destructive effect that it once did. Nothing can penetrate that cushion of the Holy Spirit. We can then step back into the family with our new identity and we can love them and bring them the same joy that we found.

When you step back into the family, you are no longer drawing your emotional fulfillment from them. You are in a healthy place now rather than a needy place. You have found your identity in Christ and you can deal with any negative emotions of guilt or fear from the family the same way you deal with any other negative emotions. You set them on the things of God.

Many years ago, I had another friend whose mother was very negative. Whenever she came to visit, she always started saying things that would create negative emotions. They would leave her an emotional mess. Within fifteen minutes she would be in the bedroom crying. One time she actually escaped from the house. She ran down to a supermarket and called a girlfriend crying. "Pray for me. I'm not going to survive my mother."

Once the Holy Spirit began to cushion my friend's emotions, however, she no longer found her identity in her family. Her identity was now in Christ and those emotions became insulated. As a result, the things her mother said no longer had the same effect on her. She didn't abandon her mother. Now she was able to be around her and love her and share joy with her. The things her mother said just rolled right off of her. Once she was free of the enmeshment, she could put her emotions, her affections, on the things of God. She could listen to her mother and talk to her. She could be on the phone with her and, instead of crying when they hung up, she could say, "I love my mother."

Before her mother passed away, God changed her and for several years they had a wonderful relationship. That never could have happened if my friend had stayed in the enmeshment.

The family may not want you to change. They came to try and get Jesus under control but He wouldn't allow it. He pursued His destiny anyway.

I can remember when my friend first got saved. She could hardly wait to tell her grandma and grandpa. She knocked on the door and went in and told them everything that had happened to her. She was so excited.

They were excited, too, but not in the same way. They got mad and actually kicked her out. They closed the door and locked her outside.

But her identity was no longer in the family. It was in Christ. She didn't abandon them but she wouldn't let them control her destiny no matter how mad they got. As a result, when the time came, and her grandma was dying of cancer, it was her that her grandma called for. All she could say was, "Where's my granddaughter? Is she coming to see me?"

She had kicked her granddaughter out of the house, but because of the love of God, she wanted her there at her bedside at the end. My friend was able to talk to her and pray with her and lead her to the Lord. Breaking free of enmeshment does not mean abandoning the family. It does mean pursuing your unique and individual destiny in God.

Biblical Examples of Enmeshment

Jesus did not enter into enmeshment. He pushed it away. He still loved His family. He honored and respected them but He refused to let them stop His destiny.

There are other examples in the Bible of men of God who had to break free of enmeshment. Abraham had to leave his family or he would have remained in the pagan culture that he grew up in and he would never have seen the Promised Land that God gave to him.

The Old Testament is a picture of the inner working of the New Testament. In the stories of the Old Testament we see an outward picture of what God wants to do inside of us. When we read about Abraham moving away from his family, it doesn't mean that you necessarily need to do the same thing, but it is a picture of the inner separation that needs to take place so that you are free from the enmeshment.

God told Abram to get up and move, to leave behind everything that kept him from the promises and the blessings of God.

> *The LORD had said to Abram, "Leave your country, your people and your father's household and go to the land I will show you.*
>
> *"I will make you into a great nation*
>   *and I will bless you;*
> *I will make your name great,*
>   *and you will be a blessing.*
> *I will bless those who bless you,*
>   *and whoever curses you I will curse;*
> *and all peoples on earth*
>   *will be blessed through you."*
>   (Genesis 12:1-3)

God says much the same thing to you. He wants to take you to a new place and bless you. He wants to bring greatness out in you and use your life to touch the world for Jesus. He wants to touch your family. Rather than forsaking them, by getting free of the enmeshment, God will make you a blessing to your family. You will become a benefit. You will be healthy. You will be able to give them what God has given to you.

God also says that He will become your defender. He will bless those who bless you and curse those who curse you. He will keep you in joy and keep winning battles for you. No matter what the devil sends your way, He will enable you to leap over walls. Nothing will be able to stop you.

In enmeshment, your life is only concerned about the family. Everything is put into the family—all your energy, all your prayers, all your focus. When you get free of that, you can step into the Kingdom of God where you now care about all families. You get an international vision in your heart to do what He's called you to do.

Abraham no longer lived in the limited focus of his family. He got free of that past and moved to a land that flowed with milk and honey, a land full of the abundance of God. He made a covenant with God in Genesis 17:9 that brought him into a new family. And that is where God wants to take you. He wants to free you from the enmeshment to your family and entangle you with Christ instead.

The apostle Paul was another man who had to break free from enmeshment with his past. He talked openly about the background that he had. It was an impressive heritage. But he declared openly that he put no confidence in it. He depended, not on his family and his heritage, but on Christ.

> *For it is we who are the circumcision, we who worship by the Spirit of God, who glory in Christ Jesus, and who put no confidence in the flesh—* (Philippians 3:3)

Paul understood how strong his background was. He knew that if anybody could benefit from his family, it would be him. Everything in his life had been done right. He was the hero of the family.

> *Though I myself have reasons for such confidence.*
> *If anyone else thinks he has reasons to put confidence in the flesh, I have more: circumcised on the eighth day, of the people of Israel, of the tribe of Benjamin, a Hebrew of Hebrews; in regard to the law, a Pharisee; as for zeal, persecuting the church; as for legalistic righteousness, faultless.* (Philippians 3:4-6)

But Paul found no success in those accomplishments. Instead, he sought to be free of them in Christ.

> *But whatever was to my profit I now consider loss for the sake of Christ. What is more, I consider everything a loss compared to the surpassing greatness of knowing Christ Jesus my Lord, for whose sake I have lost all things. I consider them rubbish, that I may gain Christ and be found in him, not having a righteousness of my own that comes from the law, but that which is through faith in Christ—the righteousness that comes from God and is by faith.* (Philippians 3:7-9)

What does Paul mean by this? He means that his value comes from being a child of God, not from being a child of Israel. No matter where you came from, it is rubbish compared with being enmeshed with Christ Jesus. That is where your true identity lies. Paul had a great heritage and a noble family. But it still was not his true identity. That had to be found in Christ and in the family of God. Paul had to break free of that enmeshment so that he could fulfill his real destiny and purpose.

The Price of Choosing Enmeshment

There is also a man in the Bible who did not break free from enmeshment. His name was Barnabas. Acts 13:1-3 tells us that Paul and Barnabas were together. They were fasting and praying with some other disciples and the Holy Spirit told them to separate Paul and Barnabas for the work to which He had called them. God had a destiny for them and it was God's plan that they go out together.

But Barnabas wanted to take John Mark with them. John Mark was his cousin and he felt a loyalty to family. It wasn't God who told them to take John Mark. It was Barnabas acting out of the enmeshment of his family.

John Mark turned out to be a disaster. He abandoned the expedition after the first stop. He changed ships and sailed away and caused a great deal of heartache and problems.

When Paul and Barnabas got back from that first missionary trip, they began planning a second journey to visit all the places where they had established churches.

Barnabas was determined to take John Mark with them again. He was family after all. Paul equally insisted that they should not take him. It was not God's will for him to go. The disagreement became so heated between them that they split up over it. Paul went one way and Barnabas went another. Barnabas chose enmeshment over God's destiny for him. And we never hear of Barnabas again.

If you do not get free of enmeshment, you will never fulfill your destiny in God. You will never know who you are in Christ and you will never have a deep, intimate relationship with God. You will never become one with your spouse. You will never learn to be healthy and you will never be able to love your family in a way that will bring blessing to them. You will miss your destiny.

God has a much better plan for your life than that kind of failure. The Holy Spirit wants to untangle you from emotional enmeshment with your family. There are several reasons why God hates enmeshment so much. First of all, He hates it because it doesn't let you be who He created you to be. Secondly, it does not allow you to fulfill your destiny and God hates to see you limited in that way. He wants you to reach your full potential in Him. You don't belong to that family. You belong to Him. And He wants you to be free and emotionally healthy.

12
Emotions Out of Control

Then the Spirit of the LORD came upon him in power. He went down to Ashkelon, struck down thirty of their men, stripped them of their belongings and gave their clothes to those who had explained the riddle. Burning with anger, he went up to his father's house. (Judges 14:19)

Samson was an emotionally-driven man. He reacted to everything at an emotional level. His life is an excellent illustration of the problems that result from emotions that have no boundaries and no controls. On the one hand, his emotions made him passionate about everything he did and the Bible tells us that God blessed him. Passion has its place.

But Samson's lack of control over his emotions robbed him of the benefits he should have had. Instead of living in the abundance that God provided for him, he lost all of the blessing and he ended up a blind prisoner, taunted and mocked by his enemies.

Anger was not the only emotion that burned in Samson. He acted like a spoiled little kid most of the time. The incident described above happened because he wanted a wife from among the Philistines. His desire, an uncontrolled emotion, caused him to ignore the advice of his parents. He nagged them until he got his way.

During the wedding, Samson got into a confrontation with friends of the bride that eventually resulted in thirty people being killed in a rage of uncontrolled anger. We all know the story of Samson and Delilah. She pestered him until he revealed the source of his strength. Even then, he didn't think he could be beaten. His arrogance put him in a place where his enemies could defeat him.

> *He awoke from his sleep and thought, "I'll go out as before and shake myself free." But he did not know that the LORD had left him.*
> (Judges 16:20)

At least three emotions were destructive in Samson's life: lust or uncontrollable desires of the flesh, mismanaged anger, and pride. Samson was anointed by God to deliver Israel. God blessed him in every way. But Samson was emotionally-driven and, even though he did deliver Israel, it brought him personally nothing but trouble. Just like Samson, when our emotions are in charge, they will bring us nothing but misery.

The Bible talks about desire in many different settings. There is a desire for good things, as in 1 Corinthians 12:31, where Paul said to eagerly desire the greater gifts of the Spirit. Those are desires that are submitted to the will of God and will produce good in your life.

The desire of the flesh that drove Samson, however, was not under any control. It controlled him. He did what he felt—and what he felt changed with the circumstances. His uncontrolled desires were emotions that ran his life. He is remembered for his great strength, yet regardless of all his power, he never learned to control his emotions.

The Importance of Setting Your Affections

The purpose of this book is to help you gain a biblical and godly understanding of what emotions are all about, why you have them and how to control them by the power of the Holy Spirit, by your thoughts and by your words. You need to get it settled in your mind from the very beginning that you can control your emotions. It is a matter of setting them in the place that they belong. Where is that? It is on the things of God. This is the theme of this book.

> *Set your affection on things above, not on things on the earth. For ye are dead, and your life is hid with Christ in God.* (Colossians 3:2, 3 KJV)

You can place your emotions, your affections, on the things of God. In fact you need to do that. If you do not, they will control your life just like they did Samson's. He did not set his emotions on the things of God and the result was disaster in his life. Emotions are not a bad thing at all. God created us with emotions and everything God created is good, but they must be harnessed and brought under the control of the Holy Spirit. They are a gift from Him to us. It would be a mistake to try and eliminate them because the fruits of the Holy Spirit flow through our emotions. Emotions do serve a powerful purpose. But the Bible also talks about the danger of allowing our desires to be out of control.

> *When tempted, no one should say, "God is tempting me." For God cannot be tempted by evil, nor does he tempt anyone; but each one is tempted when, by his own evil desire, he is dragged away and enticed. Then, after desire has conceived, it gives birth to sin; and sin, when it is full-grown, gives birth to death.* (James 1:13-15)

I often hear people say that God is putting them through a test, that He is making them suffer so they can learn a lesson or become more spiritual. They start to feel sick or they cannot pay their bills or something negative happens and right away they blame God.

But James tells us not to say that. God does not tempt people. The Greek word for tempt is peiradzo. It specifically means to test something with the intension of finding a weakness and exploiting it. That is something the devil does, not God. That word is never used in reference to God.

So God tells us not to say that about Him. Whenever we do, we impugn His character. When we are tempted it is because of our own evil desires, not because of God. Because we have not learned to harness

> Emotions demand to be in motion.

our emotions, bring them under the control of the Holy Spirit and put to death the evil desires, we let our emotions run wild. They are like a wild horse. You can try to put a harness on a horse but if he has not been tamed, he will cause great destruction. He will run all over the place, out of control, and be no good to anyone.

Emotions demand to be in motion. They are a force in our lives that doesn't stop unless we learn to take charge of them. What I want you to understand is that they can be harnessed and brought into the purposes of God. However, if you do not control them, they will be very destructive. If you do not take charge of your emotions, they will take charge of you. You can tame them through the Word of God so that when they try to become negative in your life, you can stop their motion and turn them into something good and positive.

When your emotions are not in order, then you do whatever you feel at the moment. If you feel like having an affair, you will have an affair. If you feel angry, you'll strike out at someone. It might be verbal or it might be physical, but you will strike because your emotions control you. If you look at a brand new car and you desire it, you will buy it. It doesn't matter that you can't pay your rent. The salesman opens the door and starts pointing out all the attractive features. It has that new car smell, a great stereo and it goes really fast. The emotions start to well up in you and give you a high and, of course, the salesman promises you that he can work out some sort of payment arrangement and the next thing you know, you're signing a contract. You bought a car you can't afford just because you let your emotions drive you instead of letting the Spirit lead you.

Years ago, before God directed me into full-time ministry, I was a nurse. When I was in nurse's training, we were not allowed to work on the floor where they treated people for alcoholism and drug abuse. This was because they had a problem with the girls running off with the men who were patients. Addictions are the result of allowing evil desires to go uncontrolled and those who became addicted spent their whole lives living in the area of emotions, getting that high. These addicts were also adept at drawing those desires out in others around them and it became a huge problem with some of the young girls who had never learned to control their emotions, either. As a result, we were all banned from that floor.

James tells us the outcome of uncontrolled desires. When evil desire has conceived, it gives birth to sin. When sin is fully grown, it gives birth to death. At the time of this writing, there was a story in the news from Hayward, Wisconsin, the area that I am from. It involved a deer hunter who got into an argument because he was

> Addictions are the result of allowing evil desires to go uncontrolled.

hunting on private property and was told to leave. He was a man with a wonderful family and no prison record. Yet, in the heat of an argument, he shot and killed six people. Because he never tamed his emotions, he destroyed those families, his own family and the rest of his life.

This is an extreme example, but it demonstrates what I mean. This man's emotions got out of control. He could not reel them back in. His emotions were running wild, bouncing off the walls. It happens so often in people and results in that murder, that road rage. God created you for a purpose and you will only find happiness in life if you are living in that purpose. When your emotions are uncontrolled, your desires will lead to sin and the sin will cause the death of your purpose and your dreams.

Uncontrolled Desire

Emotions rise out of our desires and uncontrolled emotions rise out of the desires of the flesh. The result is the works of the flesh.

> *The acts of the sinful nature are obvious: sexual immorality, impurity and debauchery; idolatry and witchcraft; hatred, discord, jealousy, fits of rage, selfish ambition, dissensions, factions and envy; drunkenness, orgies, and the like. I warn you, as I did before, that those who live like this will not inherit the kingdom of God.* (Galatians 5:19-21)

Each one is tempted when he is drawn away by his own evil desires and enticed and the result is sin and the acts of the sinful nature. If you are driving along and someone cuts you off, then you might experience road rage inside. When we hear of people being shot on the freeway, it is uncontrolled emotions that are the problem. At that moment, in the passion of the moment, that person had no control and so he ruined his own life and the lives of others.

Uncontrolled emotions always result in abuse. When a father sexually abuses his daughter or a mother has fits of rage and violence in the home, it is uncontrolled emotion at work, producing the acts of the sinful nature. These things occur because the person does not take charge of his or her emotions and bring them under the control of the Holy Spirit and get to the root of the problem. When the emotion of anger is not brought under control, it can explode into verbal abuse. A

> **Emotional patterns are learned as a child.**

person's emotions might build over time until he or she just lets it all out at once and, in one moment, wipes out everyone around. It feels good to that person, so he or she just goes on about business, but he or she leaves a devastated family behind.

Anger does not have to be explosive but it can be implosive instead. People try to control it by burying it. That unmanaged anger is like a bomb that explodes on the inside of them. It causes them to hold on to the offense and it grows inside of them and the unforgiveness eats away at them until it destroys their relationships and dreams. Stuffing anger can be just as destructive as letting it explode. It has to be brought under control so that the person can forgive and forget, and let go of the situation.

Emotional patterns are learned as a child. If children are allowed to have fits of rage when they are little, it will be more difficult for them to learn to control their emotions when they are adults. If they are permitted to act any way that they want to when they are young, they will act any way that they feel when they get older. By contrast, if they are taught self-control when they are young, they will be able to control their emotions when they are older. I'm not talking about burying their emotions to manage them. I am talking about learning to control them.

This does not mean that if you were not taught as a child to control your emotions then there is no hope for you. You can learn control now—and you need to if you are to move into the life that God wants you to have. Psychologists spend a massive amount of time (and collect ridiculous amounts of money) trying to tell people it is not their fault that they lose control. Of course the patients don't get much better and the problems don't go away until they deal with the real cause. Their emotions are out of control. Your emotional state may be the result of the way you were raised and it may not be your fault, but it will still destroy your life if you don't get it under control. You are responsible for your future.

If you do not learn, then every time a bad situation comes along, it will be as though it is trying to lock you up in prison. Something of the flesh wants to put you in jail so that you do not have the freedom to live as God wants you to live.

You can escape, however. You have the keys available to open the prison and get out. Those keys are what I want to show you so that you can be free. God never intended our emotions to control us, but rather to enhance us so that we can experience the abundant life of God.

Samson did not have to be the way he was. The Bible has many examples of people who learned to control their emotions, did the right thing and became great men and women of God.

Scripture tells us that we not only can control emotion, but we need to if we are to live in the destiny God has called us to. If we learn to walk in obedience to the Holy Spirit, we will not walk in obedience to our emotions. Our goal is to move into a life that is no longer emotionally-driven but rather Spirit-led.

Conclusion

It is amazing how much Christians avoid talking about emotions. We talk about faith. We talk about salvation. We talk about heaven and hell. We talk about healing and deliverance. We talk about everything but emotions. When we define how a human being is put together, we describe ourselves as being made up of mind, will and emotions, yet we focus on the mind and the will and ignore the emotions as though there is something wrong with them.

But the truth is that we were made in the image of God and He has emotions. He feels love toward us. He feels passion for His children. He feels anger when anything comes against His people. He feels joy when we do well. God feels emotions Himself.

We were created with emotions and they exercise more influence over us than any other part of our being. It is time that we quit ignoring them and recognize that they serve a great purpose in our lives. God put them there for a reason. They act as a link to faith and they help to bring us into the promises and the blessings of God. Emotions are a good thing.

The problems come when emotions are not in their right place. We have to take charge of them. We have to bring them under the control of the Holy Spirit. We have to set our affections on the things of God.

You are the only one who can do that in your life. You have to be the one who sets your emotions where they belong. You have to set them where God says that they belong. You cannot be caught up in worry and anxiety. The Bible says to let not your heart be troubled. You choose to bind your emotions to the Word of God.

You choose where to place your emotions. If you allow your emotions to be dictated by the circumstances, then your emotions will control your life. But if you choose to place them where the Word of God says to place them, you can turn them into a great tool for linking you to faith and to God. You can choose to rejoice. You can choose to praise God. You can choose to be positive.

It is not just a matter of feeling better. It is a matter of destiny. If you do not have control of your emotions, you will never fulfill you destiny. You will be unstable and unsettled all the time. You will be the kind of person that James talked about, someone whose whole life changes every time some circumstance changes.

That man should not think he will receive anything from the Lord; he is a double-minded man, unstable in all he does. (James 1:7-8)

You have the power to harness your emotions and live in the place that God wants you to live—in joy, peace, patience, goodness, kindness, gentleness, faithfulness and love. That is where life and passion are. That is where you can really enjoy life the way God wants you to. That is where you can serve Him with true passion, not just with religious ritual. Life is so much better with healthy emotion. You can start every day with the emotions God made for you. You can stop being emotionally driven and start being Spirit-led. The choice is yours.

Make a joyfull shout to the LORD, all you lands!
Serve the LORD with gladness;
Come before His presence with singing.
Know that the LORD, He is God.
It is He who has made us, and not we ourselves;
We are His people and the sheep of His pasture.
Enter into His gates with thanksgiving,
And into His courts with praise.
Be thankful to Him, and bless His name.
(Psalm 100:1-4 NKJV)

Featured Products by Winword Authors:
Dr. C. Thomas Anderson
Pastor Maureen Anderson
Scot Anderson

Becoming a Millionaire God's Way

Making Impossibilities Possibble

Making Your Marriage a Love Story

Confessing God's Word

More Than A Dad

Discovering The Power of Confession

These and many other books, tapes and CD's are available
from Living Word Bible Church. Order online at:

www.winners.tv

Or contact us at:
1-888-4WORDTV (1-888-496-7388)